YES, IT'S HOT IN HERE

YES, IT'S HOT IN HERE

Adventures *in the* Weird, Woolly World *of* Sports Mascots

AJ MASS

RODALE.

Rodale books may be purchased for business or promotional use or for special sales. For information, please write to:
Special Markets Department, Rodale, Inc., 733 Third Avenue, New York, NY 10017

Printed in the United States of America

Rodale Inc. makes every effort to use acid-free ∞, recycled paper ♻.

Book design by Elizabeth Neal

Library of Congress Cataloging-in-Publication Data is on file with the publisher.

ISBN: 978-1-62336-003-0 hardcover

Distributed to the trade by Macmillan

2   4   6   8   10   9   7   5   3   1   hardcover

We inspire and enable people to improve their lives and the world around them.
rodalebooks.com

CONTENTS

Growing up to be a huge sports fan isn't something that happens by accident. It's an obsession that gets passed down from generation to generation, father to son.

This book is dedicated to the memory of my father, Gabe, who always said yes when I asked to stay up to watch just one more inning.

The book is also dedicated to the memory of my father-in-law, Bill Grunstein, because fathers can pass on a love of sports to their daughters, too.

CHAPTER ONE

Approach the President
and We Go for the Kill Shot

I CAN FEEL THE ELECTRICITY IN THE AIR. Actually, I don't only feel it, but see it and smell it as well, and I'm trying my best to stay out of its way. The Shea Stadium I'm entering on the evening of April 15, 1997, is not the same one I left the night before. A bevy of carpenters and electricians is busy installing metal detectors at every possible entryway, and the smell of newly installed outlets—acrid burning metal— causes me to pull my jacket up over my nose and mouth to avoid choking on the fumes. Sparks dance above the large, boxlike devices, whose unexpected presence produces the illusion that I have taken a wrong turn on my way to the stadium and somehow ended up at LaGuardia Airport instead.

Finally, the craftsmen finish their work and run off, presumably to yet another checkpoint, where another juiceless machine requires their magic touch. On a normal game night, I'd simply wave to Officer Murphy, who works the door, and jump on the elevator that takes me to the press level. This is definitely not normal, though. I wait patiently in a steadily growing line for close to twenty minutes before finally getting a chance to flash my Mets' identification card and get frisked by the cops. Yes, tonight is no ordinary game at Shea Stadium, as President Bill Clinton is going to be in attendance. It's going to be a long, eventful night.

Only twelve thousand fans managed to make it out to Shea last night to see the Mets lose to the San Francisco Giants 3-2. The allure of a Dave Mlicki versus Osvaldo Fernandez pitching matchup obviously wasn't enough to overcome the home team's awful start to the season. While I didn't actually keep track, I think I managed to shake hands with each and every person in attendance by the time that game was over, possibly even by the sixth inning. Tonight's game would be a different story, though. The game is sold out, but not because fans are all aflutter over Armando Reynoso taking on Ismael Valdéz and the Los Angeles Dodgers. Certainly the Dodgers always draw well in New York, given their Brooklyn roots, but that alone doesn't account for the extra forty thousand people in the seats.

What makes April 15, 1997, so special is that it's the fiftieth anniversary of Jackie Robinson's first major league baseball game. Even someone with only a passing interest in the sport can understand the importance of Robinson's debut with the Brooklyn Dodgers, which marked the end of segregation in major league baseball. Baseball's acting commissioner, Bud Selig, is scheduled to make a presentation to Rachel Robinson, Jackie's widow, on the field after the fifth inning of the game. Recognizing Jackie's importance to the history of not only the sport, but also the country, President Clinton had requested that he, too, be allowed to say a few words in remembrance of Jackie and his achievements.

But even though the commander in chief is in attendance, and the Mets–Dodgers game is in many ways playing second fiddle to the pomp and circumstance surrounding his visit, for the New York Mets' beloved mascot, Mr. Met, the show must go on! As on any other day, I get dressed in my costume and head out to the field for my usual pregame shenanigans. The only problem is that between me and the green grass of the baseball diamond there's one of those newly installed checkpoints, and Mr. Met's head is not only too big to fit through the metal detector, but also has just enough screws and washers and other tiny metal fragments inside of it to trigger the handheld wand that the operator uses to make sure I am "safe" to allow passage.

Of course, once the wand starts beeping, the police officers alongside the machine can't resist taking the opportunity to have a little fun. They ask me to "assume the position" and pretend to treat me as though I have just been caught robbing a bank. They laugh and proceed to vigorously pat me down, then take out their handcuffs and brandish their batons before eventually tiring of the charade, patting me on the rear, and allowing me to go on my way. After taking only a few steps, I hear a young child call my name and turn to wave. It is then that I notice the man in the dark suit looking in my direction. He is clearly not amused by what has just taken place. Quite frankly, the way he's staring at me sends a chill down my spine, so I quickly move onto the field and away from his icy glare.

Prancing and dancing around, signing autographs by the dugout— no easy feat, given the bulky four-fingered mittens that pass for Mr. Met's hands, but it's a skill I've come to master over time—and posing for pictures, I lose myself in my work. This is always my favorite part of the job, interacting with the fans, particularly kids, and getting them to smile. I finish my fifteen minutes on the right-field line and make my way over to the third-base side of the field, where Jimmy Plummer intercepts me.

Jimmy Plummer is the Mets' director of promotions, and usually if he approaches me on the field it's because a corporate sponsor is standing nearby and wants a photo op, or he wants to let me know that he expects me to visit a particular luxury box as soon as possible. As is typical from a member of management, Jimmy never actually speaks to me as if he's talking to a college-educated co-worker who just happens to be dressed up in a mascot costume, but rather as though he's talking to a mentally challenged grade-schooler.

"Now, Mr. Met . . . tonight is a special night, okay?" Plummer explains in an annoying singsong. "And we don't want to do anything to disrespect anyone. Now, Mrs. Robinson will be here soon. Do you know who that is?"

This is the start of my fourth season on the job, and I've just been given a desk in a shared office on the press level of the stadium. If Jimmy had any concerns, he had ample opportunity to stop on by or pick up the phone and leave me a voicemail. In a way, it's sort of a compliment. Even people who work alongside me on a daily basis don't see "AJ in a costume," but rather the childlike personality of Mr. Met.

"She's a very important lady, and we don't want to do anything to embarrass her," Jimmy says. "Don't you bother her! You understand, Mr. Met?"

I'm not sure what Jimmy fears I might do. It's not like I have a track record of over-the-line mischief and mayhem. I'm not hiding a whipped cream pie behind my back, waiting for my golden opportunity to show Rachel Robinson who's boss.

Jimmy Plummer has clearly fallen into the trap of forgetting that there's an actual "Mister" inside of Mr. Met. Since I fail to make any wild gesticulations in his direction, I guess he considers my response to be one of agreement that I won't do anything to bother our esteemed guest. But no sooner does Jimmy move on than a female voice rings out from the stands.

"Yoo-hoo, Mr. Met! Over here!"

It's Rachel Robinson, sitting in the front row of the VIP section of box seats, and she beckons me over. With great glee, I run to her and she gives me a big bear hug of an embrace. "There's the man I've been waiting to see," she proclaims, the smile on her face rivaling the size of Mr. Met's own monstrously large grin. "I simply have to have a picture!"

She looks around for someone on the field who can take her

photo and finally spots someone she recognizes. "Mr. Plummer! Could you take my picture with this handsome gentleman?"

"Absolutely, Mrs. Robinson. Whatever you need."

Jimmy takes her camera and snaps a few pictures of the two of us, taking extreme care not to make eye contact with me when he's done. Mrs. Robinson gives me a big kiss and we hug again before I continue on my way. Put that in the pantry with your cupcakes, Jimmy!

* * *

ONCE THE NATIONAL ANTHEM IS OVER, I join up with the cameraman and a pair of my "bodyguards"—two cute college gals who are doing their best to get through a summer internship by exerting as little effort as possible—and head toward the elevator that will take us to the upper deck.

As we walk, I prepare a revised route in my head: upper deck, down the ramp to the press level and through the Diamond Club, with the cover that we have to check in with Vito Vitiello, the head honcho of the scoreboard control room, who's responsible for directing all of the in-game video and entertainment. We have no need, in reality, to go that way, but our story is plausible and the route just so happens to lead us right past President Clinton's box, where we can easily ask whoever's guarding the door if we can come in for a quick visit. The goal, of course, being the holy grail for all mascots—a photo op and meet and greet with a sitting president. I have no illusion that this will actually work, but buoyed by my experience with Rachel Robinson, I figure it's worth a try. What do I have to lose?

We pass through two more checkpoints, and the comedy routine "Mr. Met is a fugitive from justice" plays itself out again both times. However, at the second checkpoint, there's a fairly long line that stretches out longer and longer as our extended pantomime progresses. While the crowd is highly amused by the antics, there's one person who fails to see the humor. The man in the dark suit is there. I notice this time that he's talking to someone via a tiny microphone on his lapel and listening through an earpiece neatly camouflaged to blend in with his hair. There's no doubt in my mind that he's Secret Service.

His back turned to us, the man in the dark suit extends his arm in our path, and we pause while he finishes up his conversation. He then wheels around and speaks to us in a very businesslike fashion. "Mr. Met," he says, "here's the deal. You do whatever it is you normally do and go about your business as usual. We won't bother you anymore. I've made it clear that you no longer need to be searched at the checkpoints. Okay?"

I slowly nod my head, though not because of any mascot code of silence—no mascot worth his salt is going to be heard talking while in costume—but rather because this man exudes such an aura of authority when he speaks that I simply can't muster up the courage to make even the slightest sound.

"Now listen to me very carefully," he goes on, and as he continues to speak, he does something that nobody else has ever done in all my years as Mr. Met. He isn't looking up, as everyone automatically does when talking to me. Most people, out of habit, make eye contact with the person they are talking to, even if the person appears to be a giant living baseball. I've gotten used to seeing people's necks when they address me, as they crane to meet what appears to be my gaze.

But the man in the dark suit is staring directly into the recess of Mr. Met's mouth, knowing full well that even though he isn't able to see inside, it's exactly where I am looking out from. It's hard to explain how utterly creeped out I am by this. The closest thing I can compare it to is the opening scene of the movie *Scream*, in which

Drew Barrymore's character answers what she thinks is a harmless crank call and the strange voice on the other end innocently asks her what her name is. When she playfully asks why he wants to know, the voice says menacingly, "Because I want to know who I'm looking at!" In an instant, Drew knows she's in a whole lot of trouble. That's exactly the vibe I'm starting to get from the man in the dark suit. Needless to say, he has my full attention.

"We have snipers all around the stadium, just in case something were to happen," he says. "Like I said, do whatever it is you normally do. Nobody will bother you. But approach the president, and we go for the kill shot. Are we clear?"

He pauses for a moment to let the words sink in, and it feels like he isn't only looking into my eyes, but also into my very soul with his blank, unblinking stare. Then he says the same thing again, only a little bit slower this time, making sure I know his warning is not in any way to be misconstrued as some sort of gag. He's dead serious, and if I don't believe him, then I'll be dead—seriously.

"Approach the president, and we go for the kill shot," he repeats. "ARE—WE—CLEAR?"

* * *

THERE'S A CERTAIN WEIRDNESS to being a major league mascot. Mascots exist in a limbo that's very hard to describe to anyone who hasn't experienced it for themselves.

On one hand, you're a part of the crowd, able to mingle with the fans who, like you, wear the uniform of the home team proudly, feeling the joy of every victory as well as the sting of each defeat. And yet, the mascot is also allowed to venture past the barriers that separate the spectators from the players on the field without fear of being tased by an overexuberant security guard and escorted away in handcuffs. To the average fan, the mascot is part of the team itself, and a very accessible part at that. As such, your appearance in the stands brings with it a sense of excitement, hugs and high-fives, requests for autographs and for pictures to be taken. Conversely, depending on the allegiance of the fan in question—and their level of sobriety—your appearance may also make you the target of abuse, both verbal and physical. Not to mention the ever-present need to protect certain, shall we say, "delicate" areas of your anatomy from the potential attack (intentionally or not) of younger children who reside just below your line of sight.

Yet the vast majority of mascots are not part of the team at all. Mascots do not get a chance to "bond with their teammates" on road trips. They do not hang out with the guys after the game. In most cases, the players wouldn't be able to pick the mascot out of a lineup if they weren't wearing their costume, and even then some of the less-attentive athletes might fail in the task. Essentially, behind the scenes, the mascot performer is completely invisible to the very same athletes they may just have interacted with moments before on the field.

When I was Mr. Met, I wasn't issued a locker between John Franco and Bobby Bonilla, as some people might imagine. I wasn't even allowed beyond the clubhouse door. Instead, I was relegated to the old Jets' locker room, long since deserted and left in a state of disrepair after the football team left Flushing to shack up with the New York Giants at the Meadowlands in 1984.

Of course, that room was not mine alone. For starters, half of the room was overrun with obsolete exercise equipment long ago replaced and removed from the Mets' clubhouse. The other half was used as a holding area for pregame guests, such as national anthem singers, who needed a place to hang out until it was their time to take the field.

In order to afford the mascot a modicum of privacy, the Mr. Met costume was stored in a tiny closet-sized cubicle where I could change and lock up my personal possessions while I was out and about. Of course, even that sanctuary needed to be shared with the Diamond Club hostesses, who evicted me when they needed to change from street clothes into their game-day blazers and then back again when their shift had ended.

I never knew exactly who or what I would see waiting there when I arrived before each game. Sometimes it would be a gaggle of grade-schoolers preparing to sing "The Star Spangled Banner." Once in a while I would find myself unable to enter the room at all because the space had been usurped by the Mets' general manager, Steve Phillips, for an impromptu press conference.

Nothing, however, could have prepared me for the shocking image that awaited me after a "Hollywood All-Stars" celebrity softball team played a three-inning exhibition contest on the field before the regularly scheduled Mets game. Dressed as Mr. Met, I rounded the corner after a long hour spent visiting several children's birthday parties in the stadium.

There, in the center of the room, having a casual conversation, were actors Fisher Stevens, Gregory "Gonzo" Harrison, Robert Hegyes (of *Welcome Back, Kotter* fame), and musician Branford Marsalis—all in a clothing-free pre-shower state. In life, your eyes encounter certain things that you simply cannot unsee. A naked Epstein is one of those things. The horror! The horror!

Of course, sometimes a mascot's invisibility gives you a chance to witness events that truly touch you as well. On June 24, 1994, Dwight Gooden was getting absolutely shellacked by the Pittsburgh Pirates. With one out in the sixth inning, Gooden was pulled from the mound, trailing 7-1, to a chorus of boos from the disappointed crowd.

I just happened to be standing there as Gooden emerged from the runway between the dugout and the clubhouse. Gooden's son, whom we all referred to as Baby Doc, had been watching the game on a television in the day care room, where the players' kids stayed during games, one door down from the Jets' locker room. He ran down the hallway to greet his father and gave him a big hug. "You'll get 'em next time, Daddy," he declared, and as he did so, Gooden made eye contact with me for a brief moment.

Clearly embarrassed, Gooden quickly looked away and then, without a word, left his son and entered the Mets' clubhouse. Sadly, there was no "next time" for Gooden with the Mets. Within a week, news of two failed drug tests would make national headlines and the pitcher would be suspended for sixty games due to the infractions. He would fail another drug test during the suspension, resulting in his being banned for the entire 1995 season.

* * *

YOU JUST NEVER KNOW when your time will come. For me, it was 1997, which ended up being my last season as Mr. Met, and not by choice. In December I received an e-mail telling me that the team had decided to hire somebody else to be the mascot. Just like that, I was out of a job.

But even though they had taken me out of the Mr. Met suit, I couldn't manage to get Mr. Met out of me. After four years in the costume I was no longer the same person, and when I was finally able to put my bitterness aside and watch the team play again, I found that I also still saw aspects of my own personality in Mr. Met, even though "he" was no longer "me." I began to wonder if maybe mascots weren't far more magical than I had ever realized.

Before Mr. Met reemerged on the scene in 1994, the Mets were a league laughingstock. But in each season that I wore the suit, the franchise won more games than it had the season before. Maybe it was a coincidence, but I can't help but think that perhaps, in some small way, I might have had something to do with that improvement.

I remember one game in late May of 1995, when I saw pitcher Bret Saberhagen before one of his starts. Bret was one of the few players at the time who knew who I was and would actually carry on a casual conversation with me. He asked me how I was doing, and I jokingly asked him if he realized that not once that season had I gone on the field to dance during the seventh-inning stretch with the Mets in the lead. After I assured him that I wasn't kidding, he laughed and told me, "I'll take care of it."

Let the record state that when the middle of the seventh inning came around that day and Mr. Met took to the field to the strains of "Take Me Out to the Ballgame," the scoreboard showed that the San Francisco Giants had no runs on five hits and were trailing the Mets 3-0. As our paths crossed, Saberhagen pointed at me as if to say "I told you."

* * *

MANY YEARS HAVE PASSED since I danced my last dance as Mr. Met. And the Mets, who somehow managed to reach the World Series in 2000, only to lose to the hated New York Yankees, have been on a steady decline ever since. Oh sure, they did almost make the World Series in 2006, but a majority of Mets fans try very hard to erase from their memory the image of Carlos Beltran taking a called third strike with the bases loaded to end Game 7 of the NLCS against the St. Louis Cardinals. Let us not speak of this again. In any event, today the

Mets have once again become the punch line to the jokes of late-night comedians like David Letterman and Conan O'Brien.

In 2009, there were twenty-one players on the Mets who were making more than $1 million annually, yet the team managed to win just seventy games. Financial issues brought about by the owners' involvement in the Bernie Madoff scandal forced the Mets to shave more than $50 million from the team's payroll before the start of the 2012 season—the largest single-season drop in player salaries from one year to the next in the sport's history.

In December of 2011, the *New York Times* reported that the Wilpon family, in an effort to raise enough cash to retain principal ownership of the team, was courting potential investors to pony up $20 million for a 4 percent stake in the franchise. Included on the official summary term sheet outlining the partnership benefits that money would buy was the sentence "Mr. Met made available for Owners at Citi Field events."

As the 2014 season gets under way, simply put, the Mets still have issues. They do have a pair of young pitchers with a ton of promise in Matt Harvey and Zach Wheeler, though the former's elbow injury may well end up sidelining him for most, if not all, of the 2014 campaign. All-Star third baseman and team captain David Wright is certainly worth the $20 million annual price tag when healthy, but a large portion of their payroll is still tied up in players like Johan Santana, who missed nearly all of the preceding three seasons with injuries.

One of the team's highest-paid outfielders is likely to be Jason Bay, who in 2013 actually played not for the Mets, but for the Seattle Mariners, until that team gave the underperforming Bay his unconditional release. The Mets still owe him $3 million in 2014, regardless of where he ends up, if he even signs with a new team at all.

And then there's Bobby Bonilla, who last played for the Mets in 1999. When he and the Mets parted ways, the club agreed to a contract-buyout deferral clause that sends a $1.19 million check Bonilla's way every year from 2011 to 2035, which means Bonilla will still be on the Mets' payroll when he is seventy-two. It's things like that that have soured Mets fans and keep them from coming out to the ballpark. Attendance at home games continues to trend downward, and all those empty seats make the public relations nightmares of the 1993 team seem microscopic by comparison.

As I shake my head in disbelief at the state of the team I used to love, I find myself once again being drawn to the smiling face of Mr. Met like a sailor to the song of the siren. I'm not sure why that inanimate piece of polyurethane still holds such power over me, and yet it does.

I know it might sound crazy, but could it be possible that were I to wear that costume again, even if only for one day, it would some-how make a difference? I feel a bit like Jack Shephard from *Lost*, standing on the tarmac, looking like a madman and screaming after Kate as she drives away, but it's true—I have to go back!

CHAPTER TWO

The Fool's Journey

"BURN THE WITCH!"

What comes to mind when you hear those words? For most people, the shout likely conjures up the image of an angry, out-of-control mob ready to end the life of a young maiden who has been wrongfully accused of sorcery. As her screams of protest rise higher than the flames that are about to end her life, the crowd continues to chant and cheer, confident that this sacrifice will end any ills that have beset their community. Yes, in 1692, the town of Salem, only about twenty-five miles outside of Boston, wasn't exactly Disneyland.

In actuality, those convicted of practicing witchcraft during that dark time in American history were not burned at the stake, in spite of the lasting perception that continues to this day. Of course that's little consolation to the nineteen people who were taken to Gallows Hill and subjected to death by hanging, rather than being set ablaze. Dead is dead, after all.

It also does little to mitigate the fact that these people were killed for little more than fear and hysteria. But that's what can happen when large crowds get caught up in a herd mentality and reason breaks down. In Salem, the stories of a few young girls who claimed to have been attacked by specters were taken at face value, and the women they accused of being in league with Satan were put on trial. Soon after, any mishap in the town resulted in the search for the "witch" who was to blame.

Milk turned sour overnight? It couldn't have been the lack of refrigeration; it had to be that blacksmith down the road who missed church last Sunday who is to blame. A stray cat showed up on my doorstep? No way that's really a cat—it must be that widow from next door, who clearly has turned herself into a cat for the sole purpose of sneaking into my house to steal from me.

It's the same kind of tortured logic that Monty Python so brilliantly lampooned in their 1975 film *Monty Python and the Holy Grail*, in which Sir Bedevere (Terry Jones) postulates that since you burn witches, they must be made out of wood, and since wood floats just like a duck floats, then if the accused weighs the same as a duck, she obviously must be made out of wood, and is therefore clearly guilty of being a witch.

In an environment like that, nobody is safe. The tiniest argument can easily snowball, with a person who felt insulted by something you said or did running off to the nearest magistrate and inventing groundless accusations of your allegiance with the devil. These accusations would be accepted as fact by the town at large, of course, evidence and common sense be damned.

It may be a little difficult to imagine events spiraling so out of control for that long in today's society, especially with the immediate and pervasive media attention that would accompany such a chain of events. Then again, the members of that very media tasked with shining the light on such behavior would likely work itself up into such a frenzy to be "the first to get the breaking news" or "to nab that exclusive interview" that camera crews and field reporters would inevitably be guilty of exhibiting exactly the same mob behavior they were trying to expose.

One need look no further than the sports venues of today for proof that large groups of people can quickly and spontaneously undo centuries of social evolution. A close call that goes against the home team usually results in, at a minimum, a chorus of boos raining down from the stands, directed at the officials on the field. In some cases, the crowd gets far more violent. In 2001, Cleveland

Browns fans became so enraged with a referee's call that they littered the field with beer bottles and other debris, resulting in a nearly 30-minute delay. Then, of course, there was 2004's Malice at the Palace, in which a minor altercation between NBA stars Ben Wallace and Ron Artest grew into a full-scale riot after a fan threw a cup of beer at Artest and he went into the stands to confront the man he thought was the culprit. The incident quickly escalated into an "us versus them" situation, with many of the fans in attendance joining together to fight the "invading" players from the visiting team. Sadly, in American society, the journey from "Burn the witch!" to "Kill the umpire!" isn't a very long one.

The journey of the mascot to American shores was quite a few centuries in the making, though. For the origin of the concept of the mascot in Europe, we have to go all the way back to fifteenth-century Italy and a man named Filippo Marìa Visconti. Visconti was the last in a long line of rulers of Milan from 1277 to 1447. At the age of twenty, he took over the title of duke from his brother, Giovanni, after Giovanni's assassination in 1412. By all accounts, Filippo was an intolerant and insensitive leader who was about as far from handsome as a man can get. Paranoid about his physical appearance and equally concerned about losing his power, rumor has it that he ordered his wife, Beatrice di Tenda, to be beheaded based on unsupported claims of adultery. In short, Visconti was not a nice guy.

However, one beautiful thing did come out of his reign. The duke was a big fan of playing cards, specifically a game called *carte da triomphi* that had recently been introduced to Italy. The game used a regional adaptation of the more traditional playing cards we are familiar with today: in addition to the four traditional suits, these decks added a series of *triomphi* or "trump cards" into the mix. Visconti, a very rich man, commissioned a deck of these cards to be made to celebrate the upcoming birth of a child to his mistress.

It is believed that this stunning, hand-painted deck, some of whose cards have survived and can be seen at the Morgan Library and Museum in New York City, was among the forerunners of the tarot cards of today.

At the time, decks of this kind were incredibly expensive to make, and were reserved almost exclusively for the wealthy and the powerful. However, as the printing press, invented by Johannes Gutenberg in 1440, spread rapidly over the continent, the mass production of playing cards led to widespread distribution, and decks began to take on many shapes and designs. Many diverse rules for all different kinds of games were invented. However, one card from this deck in particular seemed to take on a life of its own. That card was the Fool.

In the Visconti deck, the Fool was depicted wearing ragged clothes and having feathers in his hair and a long, unkempt beard. This is believed by some historians to be symbolic of the tradition of the woodwose—a mythological figure not unlike Bigfoot in appearance. The woodwose is humanoid, but hairy like a wild animal, prone to crazy dancing, and full of mystical, if not prophetic powers. The great wizard from Arthurian legend, Merlin, is believed to have lived for a time as a woodwose before rejoining society.

In early French decks, the Fool was the only card with special, some might say magical, powers. A player who did not wish to follow suit in a trick-taking game similar to bridge could play the Fool and be excused for his "bad behavior" with only a modest penalty. The person who played the Fool could not win the trick, but did get to retain possession of the card, playing it again and again as he wished until the round was over. As decks became more plentiful and more varieties were produced, this version of the Fool card maintained its bearded appearance, though in a far neater form, while the feathers in the hair began to take on the appearance of a jester's cap, reminiscent of the joker from the playing cards of today.

Around the same general time in England, a commoner named William Sommers was about to become very famous. We're talking Kim Kardashian famous. Sommers was a servant for a respected merchant named Richard Fermor. As the story goes, Fermor brought William along with him on a trip to London, where the two men saw King Henry VIII engaged in some sort of athletic competition that was neck and neck going down to the wire. When the king pulled off a narrow victory, Sommers got so excited that he leapt into the air and began a spot-on impersonation of the Duke of Norfolk that so amused Henry VIII he invited Sommers to become his court jester.

Whether or not the story is true, Sommers indeed was the official court jester for the next thirty-five years, until his death in 1560. An entire career was born out of a single moment of inspired insanity.

*　*　*

EDMOND AUDRAN WAS A composer who specialized in the style known as *opéra comique*, which combines the arias of traditional opera, where every line of the performance is sung, with spoken dialogue. Think of him as the Black-Eyed Peas of his era. In 1880, Audran's latest production was ready to make its debut. It was called *La Mascotte*, and it was set in Italy in the fifteenth century—coincidentally, the time of Filippo Marìa Visconti.

At the start of the opera, Rocco, a struggling farmer who believes himself to be the victim of bad luck, laments his fate. His shepherd, Pippo, soon returns from a journey to see Rocco's brother, from whom he had sought help for Rocco's recent run of misfortune. Instead of money, though, Pippo returns with only a basket of eggs and Bettina, the brother's turkey keeper. Rocco is not happy with this turn of events, but Pippo tries to explain that Bettina is no ordinary girl. She is a mascot.

Rocco, of course, has no idea what a mascot is, so Pippo gives him the definition in song:

> *Those messengers that heaven sends,*
> *Are known as Mascots, my good friends:*
> *Thrice happy he unto whose home*
> *These kindly angels come! Ah! . . .*
> *So, soon as in some mortal home,*
> *An angel of this band appears,*
> *A good fortune with it doth come,*
> *That drives out all troubles and tears. . . .*

Yes, Bettina possesses magical powers and brings good luck to whomever she works for—so long as she remains a virgin—which gives rise to the opera's conflict, as Pippo falls in love with her and must decide between "her lovely little lumps" and loyalty to his master.

The opera proved to be very popular in Paris, and it played for the next five years. During that successful run, word of *La Mascotte* made its way to England, where it was translated into English as *The Mascot*. Eventually, performances made their way to America, with Boston being the location of the opera's debut—and a successful one at that—so it didn't take too much time before the troupe traveled to New York City to bring the show to Broadway.

The runaway popularity of *The Mascot* actually brought the word into common usage in the United States. Soon, everybody knew that a "mascot" was an animal, human, or thing that brought good luck. It wasn't long before colleges in the Northeast started embracing mascots of their own. Princeton adopted the image of a tiger as its symbol, while Yale opted instead for a bulldog named Handsome Dan as the official good luck charm of its athletic teams. While the Yale definition of "handsome" may well be called into question, Dan is generally acknowledged to have been the first "live" college mascot in the country.

Of course, Harvard, located a stone's throw from Boston, adopted a kind of mascot of its own during this same time: John Lovett, aka John the Orangeman. He was so nicknamed not only because he had traveled to America from Ireland as a child, but also because he sold fruit from a donkey cart in Harvard Yard.

Despite his gruff exterior, the students took a liking to him, and John was given free rein to roam just about anywhere he wanted on campus. At football games, which he attended religiously, fans would decorate John with crimson streamers (the school color) to help rally the team to victory.

How ironic that in the very corner of the state that once saw alleged witches put to death because of the mere suggestion that they might possess magical qualities, the most educated of individuals now celebrated a witch of their own. After all, Edmond Audran hadn't pulled the word *mascotte* out of thin air. On the contrary, the word was a form of French slang at the time, deriving from the word *masco*, meaning "witch."

Mascots are fools. They are jesters. And yes, they are witches. In short, they represent everything that the original colonists had rejected centuries before. Yet, as the United States hurtled toward the twentieth century, mascots were quickly becoming an integral part of the culture.

In 1919, the Chicago White Sox made it to the World Series, a result that some people credited to the hiring of Eddie Bennett. Bennett was a physically disabled orphan who also happened to possess a love of baseball along with a winning smile. According to legend, he caught the attention of Chicago center fielder Happy Felsch while the team was at New York's Polo Grounds for a double-header against the Yankees. Felsch had a pretty good day at the plate and decided that Bennett was the reason, so he convinced his manager to hire the teenager as the team's mascot and batboy.

While the White Sox did go on to win the American League pennant, any potential for a feel-good story about the mascot who helped inspire them to victory went out the window when several of the Chicago players, including Happy Felsch, conspired with gamblers to throw the World Series and were banned from baseball for life.

Bennett returned to New York and the next year started to attend games at Ebbets Field, home of the Brooklyn Dodgers. Eventually, some of the players noticed him in attendance and for some reason, they were also drawn to him. As the team continued to win games, they gave the credit to their good luck charm, Eddie. The Dodgers won the National League pennant and hosted the first three games of the best-of-nine World Series against the Cleveland Indians.

After winning two of the three home games, the Dodgers went to Cleveland for the next four contests, but they did not invite Bennett to go with them. After the Indians swept the next four games, the team returned home defeated, and fans seemed to blame the loss on the decision to leave Bennett behind in Brooklyn.

Whether or not the story was true, the Yankees nevertheless decided to woo lady luck by offering Bennett a job as *their* batboy in 1921. He remained with the team for the next dozen years, a period of time in which Babe Ruth rewrote the record books and the Yankees won seven pennants and four World Championships.

But not all of the early mascots in baseball provided their teams with good luck. In fact, one in particular is said to continue to bring bad luck to this very day. I'm talking about the Chicago Cubs and the Curse of the Billy Goat. As the story goes, on October 6, 1945, as the Cubs were enjoying a two-games-to-one lead in the World Series

against the Detroit Tigers, the owner of a local tavern, William Sianis, bought two tickets for Game 4. One of them was for his pet goat, Murphy. Sianis wanted to bring his favorite baseball team some good luck by having Murphy, the mascot of his bar, the Billy Goat Tavern, with him at this important game.

Unfortunately, things did not go off exactly as Sianis had planned. Ticket takers at the gate refused to let the goat in, citing the stadium's no-animals policy. Sianis was livid and demanded to speak with Mr. Wrigley, the owner of the team, who told Sianis that while he was welcome to come in, the goat had to remain outside the stadium. When pressed to give a good reason why, Wrigley reportedly said, "Because the goat stinks." At this point Sianis was so outraged that he declared the Cubs would never win again until the goat was allowed inside Wrigley Field, and he stormed off in a huff.

Well, the Cubs lost that day, and the next, and the next. The Tigers won the World Series and the Curse of the Billy Goat was born. The Cubs did manage to win eighty-two games in 1946, but never were able to top the .500 mark again until 1963, when they again won eighty-two games. Although Sianis did publicly rescind the curse in 1969, the year before his death, as the 2014 season gets under way, Cubs fans are still waiting for another trip to the World Series.

* * *

EDDIE BENNETT AND MURPHY THE GOAT ASIDE, the modern sports mascot likely wouldn't exist if not for a man named Max Patkin.

Patkin was born in Philadelphia in 1920 and dreamed of one day being a major league baseball player. It wasn't a crazy dream either. Patkin had some actual talent. After high school, he signed a contract with the Chicago White Sox, but after two uneventful seasons pitching

in the minor leagues in Wisconsin, it didn't look as though he'd be reaching his goal anytime soon.

So, when America decided to enter the fray of World War II, Patkin gave up his dream and joined the Navy instead. While he was stationed in Hawaii, Patkin continued his passion for baseball by pitching for a service team. As fate would have it, one day Patkin found himself on the mound in an exhibition game when up to the plate came fellow serviceman Joe DiMaggio, who by 1944 was already a seven-time All-Star and two-time Most Valuable Player of the American League.

Patkin took a deep breath and threw a pitch plate-ward. Joltin' Joe promptly hit a mammoth home run that is said to have landed in the Pacific Ocean. DiMaggio began to circle the bases as the crowd roared its approval. That's when it happened. As DiMaggio rounded the bases, the crowd suddenly went silent as Patkin seemed to snap. He threw his glove to the ground in disgust and took off in a rage after DiMaggio. Only Patkin wasn't really upset. As he caught up to the superstar, Patkin altered his gait and posture to perfectly mimic DiMaggio's home run trot. Once the crowd realized what was going on, they roared with laughter.

When all twenty of DiMaggio's teammates ran out of the dugout and ignored their famous teammate to shake hands and congratulate Patkin instead, he knew he was on to something. Patkin's puffery was so well received that he was encouraged to continue to "perform" while pitching in these exhibition games.

As fate would have it, the owner of the Cleveland Indians, Bill Veeck, saw one of Patkin's "outbursts" and was intrigued. He hired the pitcher to help boost attendance at the team's home games not as a part of the team, but as an entertainer. Patkin performed his slapstick for several seasons, but when attendance figures regained respectability, his major league mascot career came to an abrupt

end. Still, Max had a gift and took to the road, performing his brand
of baseball humor for years at minor league stadiums all across
America.

It's a long journey from lucky batboys and odorous farm ani-
mals to the costumed creatures that patrol major league stadiums
today. But if there is a single person who helped to make that transition possible, it was probably Patkin. While Patkin may not have
been the first "Clown Prince of Baseball," he certainly is the best
known, having been immortalized by playing himself in the film
Bull Durham in 1988. Patkin continued to perform until 1993, when
a sprained ankle he suffered slipping on the steps of a slick Fenway
Park dugout forced him into retirement. When he passed away in
1999, relatives said the phone rang off the hook with fans calling to
express their condolences.

Patkin set the standard for what mascots were "supposed" to do,
and ever since he came on the scene, it wasn't going to be enough to
simply stand there being lucky. No, the next wave of mascots would
have to do much more than that in order to impress the masses. It
would take a high-energy performer. It would take a larger-than-life
personality. It would take . . . a chicken.

CHAPTER THREE

Ted and Dave and Night and Day

IN MARCH OF 1974, an employee from radio station KGB in San Diego came to the campus of San Diego State University. His mission? Find someone—anyone—who would be willing to help out the radio station in an upcoming promotional stunt. They had rented a chicken suit and needed a warm body to put it on, go to the local zoo, and give away chocolate Easter eggs for a week, for a grand total of $2 an hour.

Whether you want to call it fate, luck, or sheer coincidence, KGB's representative happened upon Ted Giannoulas, a student looking to make a little extra cash. Giannoulas agreed to do it, shook hands with the guy from the radio station, and was told to just show up at the zoo.

By the time the week was over, Giannoulas had learned that he actually enjoyed wearing the costume, and he offered to continue donning the chicken suit to promote the radio station at San Diego Padres games in exchange for free admission. KGB agreed, and over the next five years, Giannoulas became a fixture at Padres games and throughout the San Diego community, doing everything from delivering watermelons to people at the beach to handing out concert tickets on the street. His over-the-top performances became legendary, and even Elvis Presley is said to have doubled over with laughter upon seeing the Chicken dancing away in the aisles at one of his San Diego concerts.

The Chicken was gaining notoriety, and was bringing far more attention to himself than to the radio station he was supposed to be promoting, much to the chagrin of KGB. The radio station was getting fed up. So they fired Ted Giannoulas, and sued to prevent him from appearing anywhere while wearing a chicken costume.

The courts, however, sided with Giannoulas, and the Padres welcomed him back in style. On June 29, 1979, a police motorcade accompanied a ten-foot Styrofoam egg sitting atop an armored car into the stadium, and a crowd of 47,000 fans cheered as the San Diego Chicken, now freed from his radio station captivity, was reborn, exploding out of the egg sporting a new costume in what was billed as the Grand Hatching.

The event was so unprecedented and extravagant in nature that the start of that night's scheduled game was pushed back by thirty minutes so all the hoopla could play out, and local television stations broke into regular programming to air the proceedings live. As "Thus Spoke Zarathustra" played over the stadium's public address system and the Chicken thrust his hands skyward in triumph, the crowd cheered louder still. Members of both the Padres and the visiting Houston Astros joined in the tribute, which did not come to a conclusion until finally San Diego's Kurt Bevacqua and John D'Acquisto carried him off the field on their shoulders.

One of the only teams that took notice of what was going on in San Diego was the Philadelphia Phillies. A young executive with the team named Dennis Lehman had gone on a West Coast swing in 1977 and had seen the Chicken in action. He reported back to management how the character would take over the stadium, with the whole crowd watching him perform his zany antics rather than paying any mind to the action on the field. This was just as well, given how awful the Padres were at the time—a ninety-loss season was pretty much the norm.

The Phillies, on the other hand, were in the middle of a very successful run, dominating the National League's Eastern Division and becoming something of a postseason mainstay in the process. Team executives, including Bill Giles, who would later become the team's president as part of a group that purchased the team in 1981, had also heard players telling stories about the Chicken roaming through the stands, drinking beer and pulling down the tube tops of female fans, much to the delight of a San Diego crowd frequently made up of members of the military stationed in town.

Philadelphia had already flirted with the concept of having costumed characters with Phil and Phyllis, two cherub-faced children dressed in Colonial-era garb. Versions of the characters in the form of large statues resided on the 400 level of Veterans Stadium and would animate briefly whenever a Phillies player would hit a home run.

The on-the-field versions of Phil and Phyllis would barely qualify as mascots today. They were huge and heavy and made out of some sort of plaster of Paris. Performers would get inside the shells, strap into huge harnesses in order to support the enormous weight, and simply stand still on the field for the singing of the national anthem, after which the costumes were put back in storage until the next game. In essence, they were more props than mascots.

Once Giles authorized the creation of their team's costumed character, the Phillie Phanatic, in an attempt to catch their own promotional lightning in a bottle, the statues were sent packing. Today, they reside in the middle of Storybook Land, an amusement park in Atlantic County, New Jersey.

The Phillie Phanatic was to be a kinder, gentler version of the Chicken, with an emphasis on being family friendly. Of course, the team was going to need somebody to embody this new character, someone they could rely on to push the envelope without taking things across the line. This is the point where Dave Raymond enters our story.

Dave Raymond was an intern with the Phillies back in 1976. The team had taken on a lot of extra staff at the time because they were hosting the All-Star Game that coincided with our country's bicentennial. It was a huge undertaking that required a lot of extra hands on deck, but even with the high demand for volunteers, there was more than enough supply, so it didn't hurt that Raymond had some connections.

Raymond grew up in Delaware, where his father had made quite a name for himself. In such a small state, and one without a major professional sports franchise to speak of, the Blue Hens of the University of Delaware are the alpha and omega of local rooting interest. Harold "Tubby" Raymond had been involved with the school's athletics program since 1954, when he became an assistant coach with the football team. In 1956, he added head baseball coach to his résumé and continued in both jobs until 1966, when he took over as the head coach of the football program.

By the time he retired as coach of the football team in 2001, he had won three national championships and three hundred games, becoming just the ninth coach to reach that lofty plateau and only the fourth to accomplish the feat at one school. In short, Tubby Raymond was and is Delaware royalty. And with the Carpenter family, who owned the Phillies in the 1970s, being residents of the state and big financial supporters of the school and its football program, Dave often got to tag along with his father on those occasions when he was invited to the owner's box at Veterans Stadium.

Eventually, Dave would attend Delaware himself and play football under his father's watch. When Tubby discovered that his son had changed his major from business to physical education, he was none too thrilled, but told his son he'd feel better about the decision if Dave allowed him to set up an internship with the Phillies, because "you never know who you'll meet or what might happen."

That's how, in the summer of '76, Dave Raymond was put in charge of collecting and counting all of the paper ballots submitted by Phillies fans for that season's All-Star voting. Raymond returned the following season, too, but with the All-Star game and all of its accompanying buzz and excitement moving on to Yankee Stadium that year, he found there was very little for him to do. Concerned that he wasn't going to be asked back in 1978, Raymond braced himself for some bad news.

"I was about to finish up school at Delaware in the following year and I thought the promotions office was going to call me and tell me that they didn't have a summer job for me," Raymond remembers. "I was expecting to be very disappointed because I had decided that I wanted to try and stay with them after I graduated. As it turned out, they called me at school to say 'We want you and we're going to give you your same job back, but we want you to stay for the games because we're thinking about creating this mascot. We don't know what it's going to look like yet but we have an idea, and we just need you to tell us that you're committed for the summer.'"

That's how it started. The team didn't quite know what they were asking of Raymond, and he didn't quite know either, but he accepted their offer without even thinking about it. In retrospect, he's kind of glad he didn't spend too much time deciding. "I don't want to call it a harebrained scheme, but let's just say that on paper, it didn't look to be the greatest of ideas. I think they simply wanted somebody to say 'Yes!' because they internally realized that maybe this wouldn't be a job that a person who was paying attention would really want."

After a few weeks passed, Raymond was finally shown an initial artist's rendition of what the mascot would look like. He was happily relieved to see that it looked nothing like Phil or Phyllis. Then he was sent to the Garment District in New York City for a fitting, where he was stunned to see nothing but bits and pieces of fabric, lots of nondescript white muslin. They draped it on him, stuck a few pins in some pivotal places, and that was it. No fur. No green. Raymond didn't know what to think.

In fact, Raymond didn't see the actual costume at all until April 25, a dozen games into the 1978 season, the day the mascot was set to make its debut. But when he finally laid eyes on it, Raymond was blown away by the sight of the familiar green giant that generations of Philadelphians have since come to know and love. He followed the manufacturer's intricate directions on how to properly dress in the leggings and shoes and body and hands and head—and in what order each piece of the puzzle needed to go on, a trick in and of itself. Then he went down to the field during batting practice to give it a test drive.

At the time, there was no official name for the mascot. In fact, a naming contest had been in the works, but the team's slogan that year was "Be a Phillies Phanatic" and a giant pennant with those words was in clear view as he took his first steps in public. It kind of took on a life of its own, and the name stuck. But while naming the beast proved to take care of itself, Raymond had bigger concerns on his mind.

He made his way up to Bill Giles's office and knocked on the door. "What do you want me to do?" he asked his boss. "Nobody told me what you were expecting me to do."

Giles looked at Raymond, perplexed. Apparently, he hadn't really thought it out that far. They'd had the foresight to know that having a mascot was potentially a terrific idea, and they were brave enough to have a costume made and to find a performer to bring that creation to life. But beyond that? Giles's silence spoke volumes. Finally, Giles simply said, "Go out and have fun."

Without any announcement—the team didn't want to make a big deal about the Phanatic's arrival in case it bombed—and therefore with plausible deniability firmly in place, Raymond was let loose on the crowd. Many of the fans in the stands that day simply thought he was one of them, assuming that the curious mascot was really just an enthusiastic fan who had gone to the trouble of coming to the game dressed in a costume. The reception was amazing.

Taking his inspiration from cartoon characters like Daffy Duck, Raymond bounced around in a hyperactive fashion, kissing and hugging people and acting as if he owned the entire stadium. And it didn't take long before that was actually true.

"I'd simply try things, and if people responded to it, I'd continue to do it," Raymond said. "I'd jump over a railing, because the costume allowed me to be agile even though I looked like a three-hundred-pound Muppet, and people would go 'Wow!' I'd stand on a railing and I'd hear the crowd go 'Ooh!' I'd accidentally trip because my shoes were too big and I'd get a huge laugh, so that became part of the routine."

The Phillies gave Raymond a ton of freedom. They'd never tell him to stop doing something that they thought was a mistake; instead, they'd discuss things with him and let him come to that conclusion on his own. And just as often, people behind the scenes would give him suggestions for things to try out.

The idea for the Phanatic to join the grounds crew on the field in the fifth inning came from Giles himself. The first time Raymond went out with the gang to "help" sweep the aprons and change the bases—Veterans Stadium was covered in Astroturf except for these small dirt cutouts—he accidentally tripped one of the crewmen, causing him to fall. People laughed like crazy and over time, the routine grew and grew to the point where by the end of the season, with the entire grounds crew and the Phanatic dancing together to Count Basie's "Jumpin' at the Woodside" (a song popularized by Gene Gene the Dancing Machine on *The Gong Show*, at the time one of the most beloved shows on television), standing ovations became the norm.

Raymond was living out a childhood dream from his days spent riding the stadium elevator as a kid, hoping to bump into players like Dick Allen. Now he was out on the field with license to actually go up and shake hands with Bob Boone, Greg Luzinski, and Tug McGraw. Although he was becoming more and more of a star in his own right, Raymond continued to be a bit starstruck himself. Discovering that his presence riled up visiting players who were a bit more antagonistic, attempting to trip him or give him playful shoves as he walked by—stuff that the fans reacted to in a big way—he began to spend more time interacting with the likes of Dave Parker, Willie Stargell, and Johnny Bench.

With the team winning more and more often on the field, it may have been a subconscious connection in the public's mind that linked that success to the appearance of the Phanatic, but that perception certainly didn't hurt. As Raymond puts it, "If the Phillies had continued to be cellar dwellers, I [still] think that the Phanatic would have been successful, because it would have been a distraction. But I think we got lucky. It was definitely easier because we were winning."

It also could have been easy for the team to try to exert control over what Raymond was doing, but the organization gave him the freedom to continue developing the character on his own, allowing it to evolve over time. Raymond recognizes how fortunate he was to have that trust from his bosses. "When you put trust in someone who is not a sociopath, someone who is not going to betray that trust and take advantage of the situation, then good things can result [from it]. Fortunately, I was not a sociopath."

Raymond said he had carte blanche to try just about anything, and recalls only one time when Bill Giles ended up upset about a skit he performed. "It was some sort of punk rock thing and he didn't like it because he didn't feel it was family entertainment," Raymond said. But that anger didn't last long at all. In fact, even on the one occasion in which Giles would have been totally justified in flying off the handle, or even sending Raymond to the unemployment line, he instead chose to forgive and forget.

"Once, because I was still a kid, I blew off an appearance just because I didn't want to go," Raymond recounted. "Bill didn't yell at me. He simply fined me the cost of the appearance and told me not to ever do that again, explaining that people expect me to show up and they bring their families to come and see me. How many other organizations would have just fired somebody on the spot for doing that?"

Clearly the Phillies understood there was more to the equation than simply stuffing just anybody into the suit. They knew they had caught lightning in a bottle with Raymond, and they fostered that talent the same way they would take their time nurturing a talented rookie who makes a few errors on the field. Raymond was young, physically fit, and up to speed on the latest trends in music. At the time, the disco craze had caught the nation by storm, so having a mascot who was able to embrace a love of dancing allowed the character to connect with multiple generations of fans. "It was a perfect storm of positive things," Raymond said. "The team was doing well, and ESPN was not quite there yet, so you weren't seeing clips of mascots all over the television. People who came to the stadium had never seen that kind of entertainment before. They hadn't seen the Chicken. It just all came together and worked and it created the underpinnings of long-term success."

Of course, not everybody loved the Phanatic. Tommy Lasorda, the longtime manager of the Los Angeles Dodgers, seemed to become apoplectic whenever he saw the big furry beast on the field. In one notorious incident, the Phanatic brought out a mannequin, dressed in a Dodger uniform stuffed with a pillow to create a bit of a gut, that was clearly intended to be a representation of Lasorda. Standing in front of the visiting dugout, the Phanatic tossed the figure around like the rag doll it was, prompting Lasorda to hurl a baseball at him. Unable to contain his disgust as the Phanatic continued his abuse of Lasorda's effigy, the fiery manager emerged from the dugout. At first, he walked slowly toward the Phanatic, who proceeded to taunt him, wiggling his own massive belly at the manager. Suddenly, Lasorda charged the mascot. The Phanatic took off running, but Lasorda wrestled him to the ground, grabbing hold of the mannequin and using it as a weapon to beat the Phanatic before ultimately "rescuing it" and taking it with him back to the safety of the visitors' dugout.

Raymond remembers Lasorda fondly, and believes that the apparent hatred was simply an act. "There's no question there was a long period of time where he loved the Phanatic and he used it as a foil to have his players laugh and see him get all agitated. When that incident with the dummy boiled over, he got labeled as hating the Phanatic, but I think he just never liked anyone getting more attention than he did. I look at that stuff fondly and I've run into him occasionally over the years. He's always been very pleasant."

While the scuffle with Lasorda brought laughter to those who saw it live, there was one incident where Raymond truly did feel in danger. In 1984, the Phillies were playing their hated rival, the New York Mets. Due to the relative proximity of the two cities, a large contingent of visiting fans is typically in attendance whenever these two teams meet—especially when the home team is in the midst of a losing season, as was the case in 1984.

Part of Raymond's repertoire was to spontaneously, unannounced, make his way into a section of the stadium at random in order to play with the fans. Unfortunately, on this particular night, he was at the wrong place at the wrong time, making his grand entrance in a section in the 300 level in left field made up almost exclusively of Mets fans—ones who had snuck in a big jug full of vodka and orange juice, currently not quite as full as it was when the game started.

With their chests painted blue and orange and hopped up on screwdrivers, the Mets fans immediately began to pummel the Phanatic with wild haymakers. Being that the Phanatic was quite visible in the stadium, security noticed what was going on fairly quickly. Guards streamed into the section and, in an effort to extricate himself from the situation, Raymond threw the only punch of his career. The crowd went wild when they saw this, but it only further incited the drunken Mets fans. As the melee grew in size, people were launching themselves at the Phanatic, throwing both alcohol and punches willy-nilly. Eventually, he was able to exit the area and order was restored. But that was as nervous as Raymond had ever been in the costume.

Fortunately, minor bumps and bruises aside, in spite of all the crazy things Raymond did over the years, nobody actually ever got hurt. However, although one can get lucky and escape injuries, time is something from which no man—not even a man who has spent years disguised inside giant layers of green fur—can permanently hide. Being a mascot is not something that you can do forever, and at some point, every performer needs to start to look to the future.

In 1993, Raymond left the Phillies organization and the costume he had worn for fifteen years.

It's not that Raymond thought he wouldn't have a future with the team, post-Phanatic. The problem was that most people assumed he *would*. Upper management had encouraged him throughout his tenure to "try and learn about the business," he says, so he'd have lunches with people within the organization in order to do just that. Unfortunately, the internal gossip mill translated the meaning of those meals into "if Dave gets close to you, and if he likes your job, he's going to take that job." And so, rather than ruin relationships, Raymond stopped his fact-finding tour, which the higher-ups in the organization took to mean he wasn't interested in a long-term future with the club.

With the writing on the wall, and fearing a pay cut on the horizon if he stayed, Raymond seized upon an opportunity to become an entrepreneur. Today, he holds the title of Emperor of Fun and Games at Raymond Entertainment Group, a company that helps develop marketing opportunities and character branding for organizations across the country.

Part of his company's mission is to help train and develop the mascot performers of tomorrow, and Raymond puts emphasis on the power of fun. "The mascot is the link that helps people forget about their troubles for a time," he said. "He's the suggestion that this is supposed to be fun. I know athletes are making millions of dollars and we're supposed to be concerned about steroids and these issues are important, but when you boil it all down, people come to games *to have fun*. Unless your father is the head coach, whose job actually *does* depend on the team winning—and I've been there— ultimately most of the people come to those events to be entertained. They may live vicariously through some people on the field or they may have some love of baseball or the particular sport, but it boils down to distracting fun and no one is ever going to tell me any different. The mascot is really the embodiment of that."

Unfortunately for me, Raymond's career as a major league mascot ended just as mine was about to begin, so until I contacted him to request an interview for this book, we had never spoken. After only a brief conversation, I realized just how much I could have learned in such a short time back when I was starting out. I also learned just how willing Raymond was to share those insights with anybody who showed an interest in learning about this very special job we shared.

I did, however, have an opportunity to meet Ted Giannoulas during my time as Mr. Met, and unfortunately my regard for the man behind the Chicken lies at the completely opposite end of the spectrum from my respect for Dave Raymond. One day I came to work and was told that the Chicken, as part of a promotion for a new chicken sandwich being debuted by McDonald's, would be performing with me the following Sunday.

A midweek meeting was scheduled with Giannoulas, myself, and Tim Gunkel, the head honcho of my department, whose umbrella of oversight encompassed all areas of in-game entertainment, including Mr. Met. We sat in a room to figure out what the pregame "unveiling" of the sandwich would look like and exactly how the Chicken and I would be involved. Giannoulas hit the ground at light speed. He had the whole thing planned out to the second. He would get on the field and do this bit here. He'd do this skit at the end of the first inning. He'd do this skit at the top of the third inning. In the fourth inning, he'd do this routine. And so on, with the Chicken being front and center every step of the way for the entire game.

When Giannoulas finally paused for air, Gunkel told him that aside from the pregame, he would be allowed to do one bit on the field at the end of the fifth inning and another atop the dugout during the seventh-inning stretch. He would not be allowed on the field at any other time. None of the bits could involve a player or the umpires, nor could he bring any fans onto the field of play or atop the dugout.

Giannoulas listened to what Gunkel had to say and then repeated his list of planned bits, seemingly oblivious to the fact that he was being told he could not do most, if not all, of the things he had planned. It was clear to me that the Chicken was going to do what the Chicken wanted to do, and Gunkel was wasting his breath. It was equally clear to me that Gunkel firmly believed he had gotten across to Giannoulas the restrictions that were in place, in spite of all the evidence to the contrary.

The meeting was adjourned without either man caring to hear what I had to say, or bothering to tell me what Mr. Met's duties for the day were supposed to be. Seeing disaster looming ahead, I knew discretion was going to be the better part of valor.

When the day of the game arrived, Giannoulas was brought—where else?—to the old Jets' locker room. He got into his costume without comment and went to the field without me. I caught up with the Chicken in time for the grand unveiling of the new sandwich, marked by a ridiculously large cardboard box that had been brought out to the field filled with sample sandwiches for us to grab and toss to the crowd. The Chicken turned to Mr. Met and gave him a big kiss on the lips with his oversize beak, grabbing the sides of my face with his dirty batting gloves and leaving smudge marks behind.

I was not happy at all because I knew what a bitch it was to remove dirt from Mr. Met's white face, and I was even less enthused when the Chicken started bossing me around, telling me to "stand over there" or to react in a certain way to the move he was about to make. After all, this was my house. The Chicken was just visiting. And when he decided not to make his way back to the dressing room at the predetermined time, I left him out there by himself, knowing full well it was just a matter of time before karma came back and bit him on the ass.

It took less than three innings.

Giannoulas came storming into the locker room, removed the Chicken's head, and immediately launched into a tirade. "Don't they know who I am? How dare they treat me this way! They're worse than Steinbrenner! I've never been treated like this! I'll sue!" He screamed and yelled as he took off his costume and furiously changed into his street clothes. When he was finally done, I smiled to myself as security escorted him off the premises. Apparently, the Chicken had gone onto the field to do a routine in which he makes fun of the umpire, a bit that not only took place at an unauthorized time, but expressly violated Gunkel's instructions not to involve the men in blue in his shenanigans.

Before the Chicken had a chance to deliver his punch line, a phone call apparently had already been placed from the owner's box with the directive to "get that bird out of my bleeping stadium and don't ever let him back." I'm not sure if that edict came from Mr. Wilpon or Mr. Doubleday, the Mets' co-owners at the time, but it wouldn't surprise me if both men placed calls independently. At Shea Stadium, the baseball game came first. I knew never to even approach that line, let alone cross it with as much wanton disregard as the Chicken did.

I asked Raymond if he shared my opinion of Giannoulas and took a certain perverse delight that he did. "I've been very frank about my relationship with Ted," Raymond said. "I've never appreciated who he is as a person. It doesn't make him a bad person, but from the moment I've had an opportunity to do some things in this business, I've shared [what I've learned]. The Chicken is about 'me, me, me, I, I, I. This is mine. I own it.'"

Raymond is happy to give Giannoulas full credit for creating the modern-day mascot and opening everybody's eyes to its possibilities. Heck, there would be no Phanatic without the Chicken, and Raymond acknowledges that. However, as brilliant as he can be in the costume, his selfishness while out of it is something Raymond can't reconcile. "Ted has said, 'When I'm done, the Chicken dies. Because *nobody* else can do the Chicken the way I can do it. Nobody else understands costumes and comedy like I do,'" Raymond told me. "You know, it's the height of pomposity—and it's selfish! The Chicken is this great character that he can share with some young person and train him and let him take the Chicken on forever, but nope, uh-uh. 'It's gonna die. When I'm done, it's done.' It's a shame."

As of 2013, the Chicken was still taking his act on the road each year to ballparks all over the country. In recent years, he even appeared in national TV commercials alongside such current sports greats as Peyton Manning and Dale Earnhardt Jr. Of course, as

Giannoulas is now pushing sixty, he limits his workload to a handful of minor league games each summer, though he does his best to avoid the Philadelphia area.

In an interview for ESPN's Web site in 2002, Giannoulas said that was the only place he hated to go and made the claim that he could have been the Phanatic if he had wanted to. "Philly will never let me in," he said, "because they know I'd steal the thunder of the Phanatic. I could sell 60,000 tickets like that. But they don't want me because I'd steal that guy's thunder. The dirty little secret of the Phanatic, though, is that when they started him in the winter of 1977–78, the [Phillies'] director of promotions called me up and said, 'Ted, how do you do it? We want to start a new character, and we'd like you to consult with us.' They called me ten times that winter to consult."

Like Raymond, I have to give Giannoulas all due respect for what he accomplished on the field. Thanks in large part to his success, more than thirty years after his "rebirth," all but three major league baseball teams (the Angels, Dodgers, and Yankees) now have official mascots—and thankfully for me, the list of teams that do includes the New York Mets. But it's ironic that someone who has brought such joy to so many people over the years seems unable to be a team player behind the scenes.

For the record, I contacted Giannoulas to give him a chance to tell his story in his own words in this book. However, he declined my interview request, citing "several items in the works that currently call for my attention," and wishing me well with the project while lamenting that he "won't have the chance to take advantage of your thoughtful opportunity."

CHAPTER FOUR

Hiding under a Pinball Machine with the Phillie Phanatic, and Other Near-Death Experiences

EXCUSE ME, DEAR READER, are you paying attention? Please turn off the television and put down your smartphone, because I am only going to say this once. Are you ready? Here we go: Yes, it's hot in here.

There, I said it. Can we please get on with our lives now?

I'm not sure what it is in the human brain that causes otherwise rational, functioning people to suddenly feel the need to ask annoying questions to which they already darn well know the answers. If you make a mad dash from your car in the middle of a monsoon, you can pretty much guarantee that upon entering any room on the planet, someone is going to see you standing there, dripping wet, in the midst of an ever-growing puddle radiating out from around your feet, and ask, "Is it still raining out?"

If I had a nickel for every time some guy wearing a T-shirt with watermelon-sized sweat stains oozing from each armpit walked up to me on a hot August afternoon, asked me "Is it hot in there, buddy?" and then cackled with glee as if he was the most clever person in the universe for having come up with such an original thought, I'd be more than rich—I'd be Oprah rich.

Now, to this day if I mention to people—intelligent, college-educated people—that I used to be Mr. Met, I encounter the same Five Stages of Giving a Mascot Grief.

First comes disbelief: "Really? You're kidding, right? No? You were? Get out! Seriously?"

Then comes acceptance: "Wow! So you were really the mascot for the Mets."

Third comes jealousy: "That must have been a really cool job, huh? Wow! Very cool."

Next comes confusion: "You know, I didn't even know the Mets had a mascot. What does he look like?"

And then, the final stage, complete cognitive breakdown: "So, let me ask you . . . was it hot in there?"

* * *

WHEN I FIRST BECAME MR. MET, I felt a little bit like Ralph Hinkley from the popular early-eighties television series *The Greatest American Hero.* Here I was, handed a costume clear out of the blue, and no accompanying instruction manual outlining how, exactly, everything was supposed to work. Flying away on a wing and a prayer, I did the best I could every time I took the field, but I was severely lacking in confidence.

Now, I'm sure some people are wondering exactly how a person gets to become a major league mascot, especially in the case of somebody like myself who hadn't set out to pursue such a career path in the first place. While it's easy to imagine many kids across America going to sleep each night with visions of one day playing in the World Series, it's likely there are few, if any, who aspire to dance and prance around in a giant baseball costume to earn their paycheck. Although there certainly are those individuals out there who become their school's mascot and end up enjoying the experience so much that they do in fact set out on a quest to continue that journey once they graduate—we'll talk with some of them later in the book— I was not one of those people.

As hard as it may be to believe, even today, many people have no idea that Mr. Met even exists. When people find out that I used to be the mascot for the Mets, a frequent follow-up is typically "I didn't even know the Mets had a mascot." And in fact, until 1994, the Mets did not have one.

Well, strictly speaking, that's not entirely true. The Mets were born in 1962, five years after the Brooklyn Dodgers and the New York Giants decided to move out to California, leaving the Big Apple without a National League franchise of its own. For two seasons, the Mets took up residence at the Polo Grounds, the vacant former home of the Giants, but part of the agreement the new team's ownership had made with Major League Baseball was that in return for being awarded a franchise, they had to build a new stadium for it. And so, Shea Stadium was built in Flushing, Queens, adjacent to the site of the 1964 World's Fair.

On May 31, 1964, between games of a double-header against the Giants, the home crowd was treated to an appearance by a very special guest. Donning a small, papier-mâché baseball-shaped head and trotting out to wave to the fans, Dan Reilly, who was working in the ticket office, brought the cartoon figure of Mr. Met to life. The character had appeared on scorecards and programs since the team's inception, but now, there he was out on the field shaking hands, posing for pictures, and signing autographs. He was a big hit, and made many appearances in the stadium and throughout the community over the following few years.

Eventually though, the novelty wore off. After the Miracle Mets won the World Series in 1969, the team was no longer a bunch of lovable losers. Fans came to the park to see their champions: Tom Seaver and Jerry Koosman and Tommie Agee and Ron Swoboda. The players were more than capable of providing all the entertainment the fans needed. Slowly, Mr. Met's appearances dwindled away until baseball's first-ever "live" mascot faded into the annals of history.

Over the next two decades, while the Mets went through their ups and downs, the baseball-shaped head sat silently in storage, left to collect dust.

All of that changed in 1993. They say that misery loves company, and in 1993, no team in baseball was more miserable than the Mets. My beloved baseballers from Flushing not only lost 103 games with one of the highest-paid rosters in recent memory (inspiring sportswriters Bob Klapisch and John Harper to pen the book *The Worst Team Money Could Buy: The Collapse of the New York Mets*), but also were a public relations disaster of epic proportions.

In late July, pitcher Bret Saberhagen threw a firecracker under a table near a group of reporters in the team's clubhouse. "It was a practical joke," Saberhagen said at the time. "If the reporters can't take it, forget them." The humor was lost on most people since just a few days prior, Mets outfielder Vince Coleman had thrown an M-80 firecracker in the Dodger Stadium parking lot, injuring three fans, including an eleven-year-old boy and a two-year-old girl. Coleman later reportedly said he didn't know throwing explosives at people could result in injury. Coleman was eventually sentenced to two hundred hours of community service and suspended by the Mets for the rest of the season.

On the same night as *his* fireworks incident, Saberhagen also ran around squirting bleach from a water gun, hitting several reporters in the process. Although the former Cy Young Award winner's involvement remained unknown for several weeks, eventually a team investigation discovered he was in fact the culprit, and Saberhagen ultimately apologized and agreed to donate a day's pay ($15,384.62) to a charity designated by the New York chapter of the Baseball Writers' Association of America. While the reporters seemed satisfied with the gesture and were willing to put the incident behind them, repairing the team's image in the eyes of the fans wasn't going to be nearly as simple as writing a check to charity.

In March of 1994, I was unemployed, living back at home in New York City after a postcollege fortune-finding trip to California failed to bear fruit. I was reading the Help Wanted section of the newspaper one morning, hoping that this would be the day that something there would "speak" to me. After weeks of endless silence, I finally heard something.

Evidently, there were plans afoot to open up some sort of Nickelodeon-themed mini amusement park just outside of Shea Stadium, and they were looking for actors to participate in stage shows as well as knowledgeable Mets fans to give guided tours of Shea. It appeared the Mets were going to try to wash away the negative image resulting from fireworks and bleach with green slime.

Although I wasn't going to be winning any Oscars anytime soon, I had done enough acting over the years to make auditioning for the stage shows worth a shot, and besides, with all the time I had spent at Shea Stadium in my life and my knowledge of Mets history, I knew that at the very least I could get hired as a tour guide. I sent in my résumé and almost immediately got called in for an interview.

After filling out the requisite paperwork that a job interview entails, I was escorted into one of the suites on the Diamond Club level of the stadium. Two representatives from Nickelodeon were there, and they explained that they simply wanted to chat and get to know me better. Luckily for me, doing so did not scare them off, and shortly thereafter one of them stood up and shook my hand. "You're hired," he said. "Be back here on Monday for stage show rehearsals."

On Monday, I got my first look at what was going to be called Nickelodeon Extreme Baseball. At a cost of $1.5 million, the Mets and Nickelodeon were turning the area behind the scoreboard in right field into a place that was so kid friendly, parents wouldn't be able to resist bringing their children to Shea. There were carnival games with themes based on Nickelodeon shows like *Ren and Stimpy* and *Weinerville*. There were video batting cages where kids could pretend to face off against their favorite Mets pitchers. There was a stage for shows where actors such as myself would ask for volunteers to "get sloppy" and be covered in "gak" and "slime."

Then there was the pièce de résistance—the core attraction of the park: a three-story Guts Extreme Baseball diamond with nets, rope swings, ball crawls, and slides, where two teams of nine kids would get to face off in a game of "extreme baseball." The game required the kids to run through an obstacle course while trying to get their entire team around the bases faster than their opposition, and the plan was for there to be several games each day. We were all impressed and excited, and we dove right into our rehearsals.

The man who had hired me was there. He introduced himself to the group simply as Bob and said he was from Nickelodeon headquarters down in Orlando. He said he had extensive experience performing versions of the shows we were going to be learning, and truth be told, he did give off a Marc Summers kind of vibe, though just a tad more flamboyant. Bob then introduced us to his assistants, a pair of improvisers hired from Orlando's SAK Theater, where Wayne Brady got his start. Joel McCrary and Clare Sera were not only incredibly talented, but also incredibly generous, and more than willing to help each one of us develop a wacky persona for a character we would all take turns playing in a show called "Game Lab."

In "Game Lab," our character was supposed to wander in with the rest of the audience and pretend to have nothing to do with the show, despite the incredible coincidence that we just so happened to be wearing a lavalier microphone that also just so happened to be connected to the public address system in the theme park. We would then make such a commotion that the host of the show, Dr. Booger (pronounced Boo-GARE, naturally), had no choice but to select us to fill in when it was announced that one of the regular cast members

was sick and the show would otherwise have to be canceled. The job
from this point on was to cheat throughout a series of audience par-
ticipation events, causing the kids in the audience to become outraged, until at the very end of the show, we'd get our comeuppance by
getting drenched by a big bucket of slime.

For our troubles, we'd be earning a whopping $7.50 an hour.

At the end of one of the final rehearsals, we were called together
for a special announcement: "Anyone interested in earning a little
extra money, stick around for a minute." Bob told us that along with
all the theme park activity, the Mets had decided to also bring in
some "costumed characters" and were going to need some volunteers
to work some overtime. We all assumed this was going to be something along the lines of Disneyland, with us dressing up as characters
from *Rugrats* or something like that. But then I heard Bob say the
magic words. "And we'll need someone to play Mr. Met."

They brought a group of about twenty of us through a labyrinth
of tunnels, eventually emerging from behind home plate and onto
the field. There, on the grass behind home plate, were three enormous black crates, each one about the size of a Dumpster you'd
expect to find behind a restaurant.

Bob introduced us to Jim Kroupa, a puppet designer who had
made the costumes that lived inside these giant crates. Jim exuded
exactly the kind of granola, earthy-crunchy, hippie-dippie aura
you'd expect from someone who had worked with Jim Henson,
which, in fact, he had. He slowly and nonchalantly opened up two
of the crates and, one by one, removed nine enormous baseball gloves
that his company, 3/Design, had built. Bob explained that to adver-
tise the theme park, as the crowd was singing "Take Me Out to the
Ball Game" during the seventh-inning stretch of each home game,
the nine gloves would perform a choreographed routine—which we
would learn right now.

Bob brought over Michael Rock, who had at one time been in the touring company for Mummenschanz, to teach us our steps. That little résumé item was quite intimidating to all of us, although if we had known the whole story at that time, it probably wouldn't have been. Although Michael is a very talented actor and improviser and does have an affinity for physical comedy and miming, I later learned that as the day of his Mummenschanz audition approached, he'd had no clue as to what he was going to do. In desperation, he bought two plungers, placed tennis balls on the handles, bent over, stuck one plunger on each of his cheeks, and did a little jig. That's what got him the gig. It's an image that prevents the word "intimidating" from ever coming into play when talking about Michael Rock.

We took turns getting inside the glove costumes and discovered that learning how to walk in the park was not itself, in fact, going to be a walk in the park. In order to give the glove its shape, you had to grasp a handle located inside the first finger of the glove with your right hand and extend it skyward. Your left hand needed to hold on to the strap of fabric located on the far side of the glove, and in order to see, you needed to tilt your head at a forty-five-degree angle and rest it against your right shoulder. Basically, we had to remain locked in a capital L while trying to maintain an upright position, sweat pouring down our faces as the Styrofoam gloves we were wearing got heavier and heavier by the second. And that was just to stand still. Next we had to add the dancing.

Meanwhile, Jim had opened up the third crate and removed two giant semicircular pieces of plastic covered in white polyurethane with a bit of red stitching around the sides. After close to a twenty-minute-long process of screwing these two pieces together, he lifted it up and turned it around for us to see. It was a giant baseball . . . with a smiling face on it. It was Mr. Met.

Everyone was happy for an excuse to remove the giant glove costumes, and we all went over to get a closer look. In two years' time, this version of the costume would be replaced by a more traditional design—the one that is still in use today. But in 1994, as Jim showed us, inside the head of Mr. Met was an elaborate series of levers and pulleys that allowed the person inside the costume to move the eyebrows up and down, to slide the eyes around to make them appear to be looking in a given direction, and to make the mouth turn into a frown or a smile. In addition, he showed us Mr. Met's tongue, which could be slid out of his mouth, "for example, if one wanted to pretend to lick an ice cream cone."

Now came the moment of truth. In order to wear the suit, you needed to be no shorter than five foot eight and no taller than six feet, and even that was pushing it. You also had to be slender enough to fit comfortably inside the head and still have room to move around and reach all the controls. In addition, the cleats they had bought for Mr. Met to wear were a size 10. Somehow, that seemed to eliminate all but three of the potential volunteers: Lankford, a gangly and slender kid whose body type fit his name to a tee; Tyler Bunch, who was pushing it a bit in the size department but had puppeteering experience—in fact, if you look closely at the credits for the newest movie version of *The Muppets*, you may catch his name—which made him an appealing candidate; and me, all five foot ten, 125 pounds of me, proudly sporting a size $9\frac{1}{2}$ shoe. Essentially, I was selected as one of the three official Mr. Mets by default. The plan hatched that day was for the trio of us to alternate wearing the costume, but that didn't bother me at all.

There I was, a kid from Flushing who had had those dreams of one day making the major leagues, standing on the field at Shea Stadium. I had just been told that I was going to be Mr. Met. There was only one thing left that I needed to do. We had been warned to stay off the field by Pete Flynn, the head groundskeeper whose thick Irish brogue made it impossible for anyone who heard it to believe he wasn't, at least unconsciously if not intentionally, the inspiration for Groundskeeper Willy on *The Simpsons*. I saw him leave the field with an empty wheelbarrow, and I seized the moment.

I slowly walked to the area behind first base . . . to the spot where the ball had famously gone through Bill Buckner's legs in the tenth inning of Game 6 of the 1986 World Series. I closed my eyes and heard Bob Murphy's voice screaming, "Ground ball trickling. . . . It is a fair ball . . . . Gets by Buckner! Rounding third, Knight! The Mets will win the ball game!" Then I was abruptly brought back from 1986 when I heard, "I said *stay* off *my* field!" Pete Flynn, rake in hand, did not look happy.

But I was happy—no, ecstatic. My feet didn't touch the ground as I quickly made my way back behind home plate and hid from Flynn among the dancing gloves.

* * *

AFTER WE FINISHED HOSING OFF THE STAGE and cleaned up following our final nightly performance of "Game Lab," those of us who were staying to perform the glove dance during the seventh-inning stretch would enter the stadium and watch the first few innings of the game from the usually empty seats in the right-field corner. Once the third inning was over, we'd head down the ramp, back out into the theme park, and around to a flimsy metal gate that opened to reveal a path running directly alongside the Mets' bullpen. If you turned right, you might get hit by a warmup pitch thrown by the likes of Doug Linton or Roger Mason, who probably were less likely than any of us to be recognized by the lone drowsy security guard sitting at the bullpen entrance, save for the fact that they were wearing cleats.

We'd turn left and walk down the long tunnel, past the indoor batting cages that players from both teams would often use before games to get a few extra swings in, past the day care room where the Mets players could safely leave their young kids so their wives could watch the games from the stands in peace, until we finally reached ye olde Jets' locker room, where our three crates resided.

The nine performers who were going to be gloves had it relatively easy. All they needed to do was don some gray baseball pants and some orange stirrup socks and wait by their selected gloves until we were called to the field. For Mr. Met, the task was a bit more arduous. Two of us had to hold the two halves of Mr. Met's head in place while a third slipped inside with a handful of screws, washers, and wing nuts and attempted to secure the two halves together without accidentally dropping some of our hardware into the wires, springs, and levers that lived inside the head.

Once that was done, the person who was to be Mr. Met would don a pair of blue stirrup socks and Mr. Met's black baseball cleats. Next, you would place over your shoulders a padded harness that resembled the kind of halo brace you'd expect a survivor of a horrible car crash to sport. You'd then step into Mr. Met's body, which consisted of both of Mr. Met's puppet arms, one of which perpetually held a baseball bat and was locked in place. The other arm swung freely and was controlled by a giant lever that rose up from inside the miniature jersey and pants. The lever barely reached your waist and needed to be attached by clips to the harness in order to keep the whole contraption from dropping around your ankles and destroying the whole illusion.

Now physically unable to sit, you'd be forced to pace around in this ridiculous semidressed state and wait until the top of the seventh inning, at which time you'd undergo the final step of your transformation. You'd wait . . . and wait . . . and then wait some more. There's no clock in baseball, so it could take hours for the seventh inning to arrive, and there was little else to do but kill time. Some of the girls liked to wait in the tunnel in the hope that players would pass by and stop to chat. In truth, most of the time they were ignored.

There was one visiting player who actually did stop on his way back from the batting cages to ask what the girls were doing there, though. It was the first time his team had been at Shea that season and he hadn't yet been exposed to the seventh-inning festivities. When the girls told him about the dancing gloves and Mr. Met, he was intrigued. He came inside our locker room and was genuinely interested in seeing how Mr. Met was put together and how we could make his different facial expressions. A lot of players have public images as really nice guys, but that isn't always the truth. Behind the scenes, some of these so-called fan favorites are complete jerks. I was thrilled to discover that Cardinals All-Star shortstop Ozzie Smith was exactly as advertised, and then some. He shook our hands and wished us luck. As he was leaving, I even invited him to perform his famous backflip over Mr. Met during our dance. He smiled a big grin and declined, explaining, "I only do that at home. Maybe if this was a home game, I'd think about it . . . but never on the road. Nice try."

Once the Mets were retired in the sixth inning, it was time to finish getting dressed. While two people lifted Mr. Met's head in the air, you had to duck down and very carefully contort your entire upper body into the giant orb, being careful to make sure the giant lever from Mr. Met's body also made its way inside, along with Mr. Met's tongue, which you'd need to be holding with a free hand that you didn't actually possess. Then you had to insert the metal protrusion at the top of the harness into a slot at the top of Mr. Met's head, which would essentially lock the whole costume into place.

With an extra forty to fifty pounds of weight on your shoulders and encased in a giant polyurethane ball, you'd then walk down the tunnel to wait behind home plate until the top of the seventh inning was over. As soon as the final out was made, Mr. Met and the nine gloves would run out on the field and do the dance. We'd alternate which side of the field we did the dance on, but other than that, the routine was always exactly the same, ending with the catcher's mitt, usually played by Sam Laybourne (the son of then–Nickelodeon head Geraldine Laybourne, and today executive producer of *The Michael J. Fox Show*), doing a somersault.

The act, to us, quickly became old hat, but each time we performed there was a large contingent of fans who were seeing us for the first time, and from the roar of the crowd we could always tell that our efforts weren't for naught. Especially amusing to me were the looks on the faces of the visiting team, who would be racing to their defensive positions simultaneously with our arrival on the field of play, especially those players getting their first-ever glimpse of us. I vividly remember that Fred McGriff, first baseman for the Atlanta Braves, was so distracted by our shtick that he nearly got hit in the face several times by balls thrown to him when he was sneaking peeks at us during the Braves' between-innings infield practice. Derek Bell, an outfielder for the Padres at the time, actually stopped dead in his tracks and laughed so hard he started to cry. He needed to be physically dragged into his position in the outfield by one of his teammates.

The biggest cheer always came as Mr. Met stuck out his tongue, as the lyric "If they don't win it's a shame" rained down from the bleachers. But the high was short-lived, and just as quickly as we'd arrived, we'd have to scurry off the field and head back to the locker room. All that work getting ready and all that waiting around, all for a routine that lasted a grand total of ninety seconds.

The initial reception of our on-field antics appeared to be positive, and after a few weeks our duties were expanded to include walking around on the field and waving to early-arriving fans before the game started. There was one additional bit of feedback from the powers that be. They'd noticed that there was a marked difference in the performances of Mr. Met from night to night. Word filtered down that while on some nights Mr. Met was "incredibly entertaining" and a "dancing machine," there were other nights when he seemed to be struggling to stay upright under the weight of the costume.

There was a very simple remedy to this criticism: Lankford was no longer permitted to wear the costume at all. Tyler was free to continue in a backup capacity, but from this point forward, unless I was physically unable to do so, the Mr. Met costume was to be worn by me and me alone.

Following that decree, the Mets maintained complete radio silence, so the only feedback I received came in the form of the delighted laughter of the fans in the seats. However, at times it was hard to tell whether they were laughing with me or, as I sometimes feared, *at* me. Like many performers who have attempted to join the mascot community for the first time, I'm sure, I felt incredibly alone. I was in need of a huge confidence boost, which mercifully came in the summer of that 1994 season in the form of an invitation to the All-Star Game.

The midseason classic was going to be held in Pittsburgh, and the Gateway Clipper Fleet, a riverboat company that provided shuttle service to Three Rivers Stadium, had come up with the idea to invite all of the major league mascots to ride their boats as a way of generating publicity. So they asked me if I wanted to go.

At first I actually declined due to my terrible fear of flying. I had been on an airplane only three times in my life. The first two flights were in 1973 with my mother—to Los Angeles and back—to visit some family friends. In addition to the lovely welcome I received in the form of the Point Mugu earthquake, I blew out my eardrum on the plane and spent the whole trip in agony. I hadn't flown again until the year before this opportunity, when I caught a flight back home from Los

Angeles—I had driven cross-country with a friend—and once again blew out my eardrum in transit. Although the excruciating pain eventually subsided, to this day I have yet to recover fully from the accompanying hearing loss.

I left Shea Stadium, returned home, and immediately had second thoughts. I was not only letting a huge opportunity pass me by, but also opening the door for someone else to be Mr. Met after that crown had just been handed to me on a silver platter. I had only been wearing the Mr. Met costume for a short time, yet already I had difficulty watching somebody else wear it. When I got inside that baseball head, I didn't just play the part of Mr. Met . . . I became Mr. Met. I was no longer a shy, quiet, and extremely self-conscious person. Instead, a part of my personality that had long been dormant awoke within the anonymity of Mr. Met, and I became bold and daring and reveled in being the center of attention. In many ways, it was like a drug, and I needed a bigger fix. I simply had to go to Pittsburgh.

Like an addict calling his dealer and begging for some help in getting a taste, I got on the phone with Randy in the Mets' front office, who was acting as point person and handling the travel arrangements, and asked her if it was too late to change my mind. She said she'd see what she could do. After a long, sleepless night, I arrived at work early and was handed a plane ticket to Pittsburgh, via Cincinnati. The following week, I would be going to the All-Star Game. Now I just had to hope I didn't run out of cotton balls to stuff in my ears.

As it turns out, the cotton balls did their magic. I landed in Pittsburgh on Monday morning unscathed and, thankfully, completely capable of hearing the representative from Gateway Clipper Fleet calling my name. Unfortunately, while my makeshift earplugs had done their job, the same could not be said for the airline. While the suitcase containing my personal belongings was already circling the luggage carousel by the time I arrived at baggage claim, there was a very large black crate that was nowhere to be found. I may have arrived in Pittsburgh, but Mr. Met had not.

After a few phone calls, we learned that Mr. Met was still in Cincinnati. The airline said that there hadn't been enough room for the crate on my second flight, so they had simply left it behind. They promised it would be the first item on the first scheduled flight the next morning. Of course, that meant I would be unable to make any appearances that day, and with only two days of scheduled appearances, that was a huge disappointment for both me and my sponsors.

Still, there was very little we could do about it, so with a promise that the crate would be delivered to the fleet's dock on the bank of the Monongahela River in the morning, the representative and I left the airport and drove there ourselves.

Arriving at the dock, I emerged from the vehicle and was immediately engulfed by something large, green, and fuzzy. When my captor finally released me from his bear hug and I stopped gagging on the smell of sweat and long-since-dried beer, I looked up to see the Phillie Phanatic, in all his six-foot-six glory, towering over me. He quickly swiveled his head around to see that there was nobody else within earshot and whispered to me. "Mr. Met, right? Pleased to meet you. We'll talk later." With that, he was off, spying a man approaching the ticket counter whose bald head clearly needed to be spit shined by the Phanatic's tongue, which uncoiled from his snout like a New Year's Eve noisemaker.

I took a few steps back and drank in the bizarre menagerie that appeared before me. In addition to the Phanatic, who I later learned was being played by backup Matt Mehler, there were no less than fifteen other mascots gallivanting around the pier, looking like illustrations birthed from the deepest, darkest recesses of Dr. Seuss's imagination. Some were characters I was very familiar with, like Billy the Marlin (John Routh), whose pointed bill could poke out an eye if he whipped his head around too quickly, and Fredbird (Tony Simokaitis) from St. Louis, whose costume tended to sag a bit, somehow leaving you a bit more depressed after seeing him than before, despite Tony's best efforts.

There were many other mascots I did not recognize, including not one, but two mascots sent from Atlanta: Rally (Chris Lee), a red furball that resembled a bloated Elmo, and Homer (Lou Stein), whose costume would soon be "discontinued" because of his decidedly non-PC Native American head, only to be replaced the following season by a character we all took to calling Mr. Met's Crackhead Country Cousin due to his baseball-shaped head and psychopathic wide-eyed stare. The reason I hadn't seen either of these costumes before, I learned, was because neither was allowed inside their own stadium—they were only allowed to greet fans outside as they made their way to the ticket-holders' entrance.

In fact, in Pittsburgh, where many of us were meeting each other for the first time, we learned that not all the teams held their mascots in the same degree of esteem: Atlanta's mascots may not have been allowed in the stadium during games, but at least the team had flown both of them out to Pittsburgh. The Expos' mascot, Youppi! (Jean-Simon Bibeau), said his organization was so cheap that when they booked his trip, instead of flying him direct from Montreal to Pittsburgh, they decided to save a few bucks by sending him to Pittsburgh via Atlanta, Chicago, Miami, and Detroit.

The days of the Chicken were long gone in San Diego, and they only saw fit to send their new mascot's costume, but asked the Gateway Clipper Fleet if they wouldn't mind hiring someone to wear it for the two days and then ship it back. That's why Bluepper, in what I believe may have been his only season of existence, ended up being portrayed by one of the college students who dressed up at NCAA football and basketball games as the Pitt Panther.

As the day went on, many of the mascots went into the private offices for their breaks, and I hung out there and started to get to know them all. In nearly every case, there was an instant bond of kinship, as we all recognized how unique our line of work was, and how lucky we all felt to be allowed to do it.

I met Dan Kilday, a dead ringer for Jim Carrey, who as Slider was fresh off his appearance in the movie *Major League II*, and Brett Rhinehart (the Mariner Moose) and Steve Amaya (Orbit) and Bromley Lowe (the Oriole Bird). When they suited back up and headed out for their next shift, in came Glenn Garry (Bernie Brewer) and Joby Giacalone (Dinger) and Mike Recktenwald (the backup for the hometown Pirate Parrot). To a man, they all shook my hand and welcomed me to the fraternity.

But of course, in every group, there are bound to be a few people you don't particularly mesh with, and this meeting of the mascots was no exception. In his human form, Trunk, the Oakland Athletics' elephant mascot, looked like a slightly shorter, overweight version of comedian Brad Garrett, and he was, both in and out of costume, an incredibly rude dude. While Trunk would usually ratchet down the intensity when there were children involved, he mostly stomped around without regard for his surroundings, knocking over whomever or whatever was in his path.

When an attractive lady happened by, however, Trunk's whole demeanor would change, and he'd swing his long, plush trunk around as if it were some sort of phallus. Out of the suit, he exhibited similar behavior. Trunk seemed to take extra delight in telling "the ladies" that his last name was Finger—which it was—but with the accompanying gesture illustrating the verb form of the word, it took an already unfunny joke to a crass and uncomfortable level.

Another guy I didn't hit it off so well with was Kevin Shanahan, who played BJ Birdy, the mascot for the Toronto Blue Jays. In many ways, Kevin is to be admired. He started as BJ in 1979, and he actually designed and created his own costume. Fifteen years later, when I met him, he was still going strong and had no intention of quitting anytime soon. Great. The problem with Kevin was that he never shut up.

Because BJ Birdy talked constantly and answered all the questions random passersby would ask him, it made the other mascots look bad when they refused to talk, as is the generally accepted code of mascot behavior. Mascots don't talk for the simple reason that it hides the identity of the person wearing the suit, so when the need arises for someone else to wear the costume (due to an illness, scheduling conflict, or new hire), the transition can be done without any one being the wiser.

From a performer's point of view, talking is also an easy way out. It's far easier to get someone to laugh by cracking a joke, or to understand that you are angry by growling, than it is to get your audience to appreciate and understand what you are saying simply by moving your body in a certain way. Being a mascot and doing it well requires skills that not everyone can pull off, and while I have no doubt that Kevin worked his tail feathers off in that costume of his, he also, in my mind, took an unacceptable shortcut.

Anyway, after several hours spent helping out the Gateway Clipper Fleet staff as an extra set of eyes for my friends in fur, it was time to call it a day. The costumes were packed away in giant duffel bags and placed under lock and key until the morning, and we were driven to our hotel. Later that night, a large group of us decided to go out to a local bar that we had heard through the grapevine was hosting a party some of the All-Stars were allegedly going to attend. When we got there, there was a huge line already out the door, but thanks to our MLB credentials, the bouncers were more than happy to let us in.

Matt (Phillie Phanatic), Glenn (Bernie Brewer), and I managed to make our way to a few empty tables way in the back of the bar, by the pinball machine. We ordered drinks and started to get to know each other a little better by sharing war stories from our on-the-job experiences in costume. I learned that Matt had only recently become the backup Phanatic, having joined the Phillies after Dave Raymond, who had just decided to retire the year before, had handed the primary responsibilities of the job over to Tom Burgoyne, his understudy for close to five seasons.

I was also told that Burgoyne and Tom Mosser, the "official" Pirate Parrot, were both in town working exclusive meet and greets with major league VIPs, which was why our paths were not going to cross this time around. It appears that when teams invest in more than one costume, they quickly learn that their mascots can, in fact, be in two places at once—so very often, they are, giving the team the ability to double book mascot appearances and bring in revenue twice as fast as less-visionary franchises.

I didn't get to learn much about Glenn's history as Bernie Brewer, because the man didn't know how to sit still. He was constantly "seeing a player he knew" and running off to say hello, only to return moments later, each time having either been mistaken or just too late. As the bar was getting more and more crowded, each subsequent departure was more and more difficult for him to navigate. Matt and I continued to try and talk above the ever-increasing cacophony around us, taking our cue to pause when Glenn's next round of "Excuse me. Pardon me. Coming through" caught our ears.

After about an hour of this routine, Glenn, struggling to make his way back to our table, caused a chain reaction in the crowd. As if we were watching some bizarre Rube Goldberg creation come to life, we watched as Glenn ducked down and another patron lifted his drink in the air to avoid spilling it, which caused the passing waitress to quickly spin in the opposite direction to avoid his upraised arm. Her tray banged into the back of a woman who had just gotten up from her chair and beer spilled everywhere, instinctively causing the people in the splash zone to jerk themselves away. In doing so, one customer ended up accidentally knocking into a very muscular gentleman whose back had been turned to the whole affair and who had no idea why he had just been hit but was also too intoxicated to really care, and he started throwing punches.

That's when I heard Glenn shout, "He's got a gun!"

So, I'm hiding under a pinball machine with the Phillie Phanatic as the melee grows in size. Tables are being overturned and chairs are flying, and the sounds of screaming and broken glass grow to a crescendo as I brace for the sound of gunfire. Suddenly, the bar's bouncers swoop in, quickly identify the main participants in the rumble, grab them all, and escort the whole fight, still in progress, right through the fire exit and out into the street. With military precision, busboys and waitresses sweep the debris off the floor and reset the tables and chairs, right down to the triangular cardboard tents proudly advertising the drink specials for the night. If not for the small stream of beer flowing off the side of the pinball machine, you would have had no idea that anything out of the ordinary had just taken place—and given the speed of the staff's reaction to the whole affair, perhaps such incidents weren't out of the ordinary at all.

Matt and I emerged slowly from our hiding place and collected ourselves. We decided that we'd had enough of the Pittsburgh nightlife for one evening, and headed back to the hotel. We got there around 1:00 a.m., and just three hours later we were on our way back to the dock. Thankfully, my costume had arrived, none the worse for wear. The other mascots all looked on in amazement as I constructed the monstrosity that is Mr. Met's head, screw by screw. "How on earth do you DO anything in that?" Bromley asked, and I really didn't have an answer. The fact was, this was going to be the first time I would actually interact with fans one-on-one. I had no idea what I was going to do.

The reason we had to be ready to go so early was because the *Today Show* was doing a special live remote from Pittsburgh. They had set up their cameras on one of the boats, and we all hopped on board to take a little ride with Willard Scott. At least that's what was supposed to happen. When I tried to get on the boat, my incredibly oversize noggin would not fit. I couldn't go through the doorway to get below deck. I couldn't climb the steps to the upper deck because my head would have gotten wedged under the overhang. So, as the rest of my mascot friends enjoyed the boat ride and the national media exposure, I was left by myself on the dock for the next three hours, sadly waving my puppet arm at the small handful of people who happened by.

It was utterly humiliating, and I certainly didn't feel like an All-Star. My costume was way too big and not fan friendly at all. Sure, I got laughs from a few folks when I would stick out my tongue, but that wasn't enough to overcome the pity I received from my peers, who felt sorry for me and my completely ineffectual outfit.

I'd thought going to Pittsburgh would be an exciting learning experience, and in a way, it was. I learned that my costume may have had a lot of bells and whistles, but in the end, it was still quite inferior to those of my furry brethren. I couldn't do the things a mascot was supposed to do. I couldn't shake hands with kids. I couldn't sign autographs. I couldn't do any acrobatic stunts. Hell, I couldn't even get on the freaking boat.

Most of all, I learned that I simply wanted to go home.

At least that's how I felt at the time, but today, looking back has started to fill me with an overpowering sense of nostalgia. I still want to "go home," but I'm no longer talking about a physical location. That itch to get back inside Mr. Met for old time's sake is getting more and more intense. But 1997 is a mighty long time ago, so perhaps I should take some baby steps before writing checks my body can no longer cash.

Perhaps I should test the waters of a slightly smaller pond first.

CHAPTER FIVE

In the Shadow of the Ferris Wheel

THE TOWN OF OCEAN CITY, NEW JERSEY, bills itself as America's Greatest Family Resort. In the summer months, you'd be hard-pressed to argue with that assertion. With a boardwalk that extends along the Jersey Shore for two and a half miles and home to what appears to be more miniature golf courses than there are Starbucks coffee shops in Seattle, the town's native population of about fifteen thousand swells to close to ten times that amount at the height of the tourist season.

Rising high above the sandy beach and impossible to miss as you get closer to your destination is the town's own version of the London Eye, the massive Ferris wheel at Gillian's Wonderland Pier, an amusement park that's been on Sixth Street since 1965. The family of the owner, Roy Gillian, has been in the amusement park business since 1930.

In 1985, Roy Gillian became mayor of Ocean City, beating out three other candidates in a very competitive race, with an assist going to a mouthy twenty-five-year-old named Dean Schoenewald. Schoenewald made quite a splash during local debates, mostly for insulting the other candidates, calling them all sorts of names. As his popularity grew, primarily for the entertainment value he was adding to a race that was pretty much a foregone conclusion, more and more of the candidates saw their chances of victory fall by the wayside. Eventually, though, Schoenewald removed himself from the running one week before Gillian's victory.

Roy Gillian served as mayor for four years, and during his term he helped lead the fight to repeal the town's blue laws that prevented businesses from opening on Sundays. Ocean City was founded in 1879 by the Lake family, who were Methodist ministers, with the goal of creating a Christian retreat that emphasized clean and sober living.

The town's charter not only expressly forbade businesses from operating on Sundays, but also put the kibosh on spending the Sabbath enjoying recreational activities like going to the beach, patronizing a movie theater, or riding on a roller coaster.

Though perhaps selfishly motivated by the fact that his own Wonderland might benefit from the added weekend revenue to be earned with repeal, Gillian helped get the referendum passed once it was made clear that the town would continue to remain "dry"—free of public drinking—and tourism increased greatly as a result.

Flash forward to May of 2012, when the "dry" debate had returned to the forefront of local politics yet again. The town was in the midst of weighing the pros and cons of loosening some of its more restrictive policies. Most notably at stake in this election cycle was whether or not to allow alcohol to be served at local restaurants, albeit on a BYOB basis.

Some residents feared that this was the first step toward turning over the town to the likes of Snooki and The Situation. Ultimately, "dry" won out again, by more than a two-to-one margin, much to the delight of the current mayor, Jay Gillian, son of Roy, who was elected to the office for the first time in 2012.

Across the street from and squarely in the shadow of the Ferris wheel sits Carey Stadium, used primarily by Ocean City High School. The most famous graduate of the school, depending on whom you ask, is either Kurt Loder of MTV fame, actress Anne Heche, or author Gay Talese. Over the summer months, when the Red Raiders aren't using the field, it becomes home for the Ocean City Nor'easters, a soccer team competing in what is known as the

Premier Development League, or PDL, considered the top amateur league in North America.

Neil Holloway has been with the squad since 2001, first as a player, then as the team's coach, and now as the general manager. "The PDL is the highest level of amateur soccer you can get," Holloway explains. "Basically, you're taking the best college players and making an all-star team for the summer, showcasing their talents so eventually when they graduate, they can get drafted by MLS [Major League Soccer] teams."

Although Holloway can supplement his inexperienced roster with a few "old pros," nobody on the team is allowed to take a salary in order to comply with NCAA regulations on player eligibility.

Talking to Holloway, one does not have to guess about his British upbringing, as his accent remains intact from his roots in Reading, about forty miles west of London. He attended and played soccer for Wheeling Jesuit University, a Division II school located in West Virginia. From there, he started his career as a player for what was then called the South Jersey Barons.

Holloway moved from the role of player to coach as the team itself moved to Ocean City in 2005 and joined the PDL. "We thought it was a better fit for the community being a team like that, and that's where we are."

With an eye toward fostering a close relationship with the community, the team soon decided that they wanted a mascot. "I think nowadays a soccer game is more than just blowing the whistle and playing ninety minutes. We're trying to create a whole event and we wanted our mascot to be something that you'd associate Ocean City with in the summer," Holloway remembers.

And what better way to get the community on board with the idea than to hold a contest to decide what the mascot for the newest residents of Ocean City, the Barons, should look like.

Holloway tells me they went into the local schools and asked the kids to submit drawings. Local councilmen were invited to take part in the vote, and myriad creatures were sifted through—from sharks and seagulls to apes and pirates and even an ice cream cone or two. The winning design was finally chosen: Bobby the Boardwalk Baron, a red biplane similar to the ones that fly up and down the beach all summer long, typically with banner advertisements in tow.

Amusingly enough, it was only at the press conference, held at Ocean City Intermediate School, that Holloway learned the winning entry had actually been submitted by one of the teachers, not a student. "She was visibly embarrassed and tried to get us to change our minds," Holloway says, "but by then we had already sent it out to begin being made."

All the team really wanted was something fun that could be associated with Ocean City, and preferably something kids wouldn't be afraid of. As it turns out, biplanes don't really have anything to do with soccer, but they decided to make it work. The next step, of course, was determining who would get to wear the costume, or, in actuality, deciding who would *have to* wear the costume.

At first, Holloway turned to some of the kids who played with the organization's youth program. He'd give them a few bucks to wear the suit for the day, but few did the job more than once. Later on, he had summer interns dress up as Bobby not only on game day, but also for nightly walks along the boardwalk to build awareness about the existence of the team, an endeavor made difficult given the transient nature of the town's summer populace.

You get what you pay for, however, and when you merely blackmail interns into putting on a costume against their will, it's hard to expect much out of that mascot. Holloway certainly didn't want to continue down that path and so he quickly realized he needed a bit more certainty. "We were tired of worrying right up until game time if we were even going to have somebody to be Bobby this week," Holloway says. "We needed somebody to be Bobby all the time. We'll provide a couple of helpers and put some promotional crew around him. But you've got to do it properly, I think, and not just throw someone in the suit and be done with it. We've got to work harder than that."

Most organizations never come to that realization. They remain forever locked in that limbo of wanting their mascot to be successful, but never quite figuring out what it takes to get their character to that next level. Holloway clearly had, so I was not in the least bit surprised that when I tell him I am thinking about getting back into a mascot suit one more time after all these years, he immediately sets the wheels in motion for me to spend a day as Bobby myself.

Now, for the last four seasons, the team has had a "dedicated Bobby" so I want to make sure I'm not stepping on any toes here. After all, when I was Mr. Met, if the team had told me somebody else was going to wear the suit for a day, I'd probably have raised holy hell. But Daniel Ash, the team's director of operations, assures me that "the kid's excited to meet you."

The PDL season is not all that long, with each team playing just sixteen games, and only eight of those at home. The team is about to embark on a four-game road trip, leaving just a handful of July dates left on the schedule.

Before I climb into the suit myself, I know I want to first watch Bobby in action in order to see what he normally does. This way, I can get an idea of what the character is, how he moves, how he acts, so I can try and emulate that as best I can when it's my turn to "be Bobby."

Plus, I also want to meet Bobby and make sure he truly is in the loop and cool with me getting involved. As much as I'd like to take Neil's and Daniel's word on faith, my prior experience with management and how well they communicate with mascots makes me a bit skeptical.

So, I plan to shadow Bobby on Friday, July 6, and then take advantage of there being no blue laws in effect by returning two days later on Sunday, July 8, for a day a decade and a half in the making. I will be getting back inside a professional mascot costume. After fifteen years.

What the hell am I doing?

* * *

FRIDAY NIGHT COMES and although the game's not going to start until 7:00, I get there around 4:30 to meet Bobby. When I arrive at the stadium, there's not a soul in sight at the entrance, so I walk right on in.

Once I get past the vacant ticket window, I see a teenager seated on the ground in front of the door to the men's restroom, seemingly in his own world yet clearly waiting for someone. I know this must be Bobby, but I don't approach him just yet, knowing all too well that during my own pregame rituals, I did not like to be disturbed. I'm not quite sure that this meditation isn't part of his routine.

A few minutes later, Daniel Ash appears. The teenager rises to his feet and seems to, for the first time, register my presence. One brief round of introductions later, and Daniel leaves me to get to know Bobby a bit.

Bobby is, in reality, Max Woerner, a nineteen-year-old freshman at Lafayette College. He's very quiet at first, but once he gets comfortable being around me, he opens up quite a bit. I wonder why he keeps coming back year after year to be Bobby. After all, I know firsthand how exhausting being a mascot can get, and at $10 per hour, $40 maximum per game, the compensation certainly isn't the lure.

Max says that being Bobby has helped him tremendously as an individual. "Bobby is a risk taker, and I was not," he says. "But since becoming Bobby, I've felt more confident outside of the suit. It's certainly brought down some social barriers for me, and there are times I even forget that I'm not wearing the costume when I'm out of it."

Max also says he loves the fact that kids love Bobby, and it's hard not to feel good about yourself when you make kids happy. He hopes to eventually be a mascot at the NCAA level, but for now, he's thrilled to come back every summer to reunite with his old friend.

I ask Max if he has a good relationship with the players on the team, especially in light of the fact that he's getting paid more than they are. He laughs, having never thought about it before. "The guys do give me grief from time to time," he says, "but overall, they're okay. So, are you ready to meet Bobby?"

We walk all the way out behind the field to the small parking area where, in the back of an old hatchback, Bobby's perma-grin beams out for all the world to see. This is Max's dressing room, right out in the open, with just a thin chain-link fence separating him from the public parking area where visitors to the city pay $10 to park mere steps from sandy beaches.

Once a few interns show up, he fully suits up and we march out to the boardwalk to try and drum up interest for the game. Unfortunately, as it's a very overcast night, there aren't a ton of people around to accept any free passes. Interns, being a naturally curious species, want to know who I am and what I am doing here. When I explain my mascot lineage and how I'll be Bobby for the next game, they both express that they hope Max will learn "how to do his job better" by watching me.

Interns are also a naturally catty species, especially when they're not getting paid.

With few people in sight, we end our pilgrimage early and return to Carey Stadium, marching back through the parking lot and all the way to the other side of the field and then entering the air-conditioned high school through a side door.

Max gets out of the suit to take a break before the game starts and asks me what I thought of his performance. To be honest, I think it's average at best. There is potential there, I tell him, but everything needs to be bigger and crisper. You have to play to the back row of the stadium, not the front row. Of course, in a stadium with about eight rows of bleachers, that's not a big difference. So instead I recommend that he play to the person at the top of the Ferris wheel.

I decide to take my leave of Max at this point to sit in the stands and watch the rest of his performance from there. Max tells me he's particularly excited about the evening's special halftime show. Every year, the team invites costumed characters from all over the boardwalk to compete in an obstacle course and so far, Max had yet to emerge victorious.

This time, though, inspired by my presence, he tells me he will not be denied victory.

What a sad lot of characters it is that parades out onto the track at the half. There's a dried raisin, a yellow crab, a recycling basket, some amorphous blob called Mr. Taffy, and two different bears. Then there are the human mascots: a guy dressed up as a pirate holding a hook in his clearly visible hand, a guy in a white jumpsuit adorned with a flimsy red cape, and a bearded dude in a red polo shirt and tan khakis. What boardwalk empire each represents, I could scarcely tell you, but looking at Bobby standing there at the starting line, I can tell you what he represents at this moment—steely determination. It emanates from the suit like a high-powered laser.

As the announcer says "On your marks," followed by the inevitable "Get set," the bull is released from the gates. Not willing to allow the possibility of defeat, Bobby takes off before the announcer has even begun to contemplate forming the *G* in "Go!"

Off like a flash goes Bobby, ignoring all the obstacles in his way and instead making a beeline for a garbage can (an actual garbage can, not the recycling basket who's competing in the race). Hoisting the can over his head as if he is possessed by the spirit of Andre the Giant, he body-slams it behind him, causing all of the other racers to scatter.

From there, it's a simple task to strut his way to the finish line and claim his first-ever win in the annual steeplechase, basking in the glory of the hometown fans who begin to chant his name in unison. Or at least the three or four people who are still paying attention do.

I have to admit I am proud of Max. While he may have acted recklessly, the truth is that he played it big. And I'm not the only one who's noticed. As I leave the stadium for the night I pass Daniel, who turns to me and says, "I don't know what got into him tonight, but maybe we should have you around all the time. It's certainly lit a fire under his rear."

* * *

SUNDAY COMES AND IT'S FINALLY TIME for *me* to get in the suit. I grab the old tools of the trade: a bandanna to keep the sweat from dripping into my eyes, a T-shirt and shorts, and a wet towel to put around my neck to help me keep cool. My wife, Sara, and my son, Xander, have come along to witness the event, to take some photographs, and to enjoy the sight of me in a mascot costume for the first time.

Technically speaking, my wife had been to Shea Stadium during the time I was Mr. Met, but that predated the two of us dating. So this is indeed the first time she actually *knows* it's me inside the costume making a fool of myself. And still she's here. It's good to know she truly loves me.

To the back of the station wagon we go. I step into Bobby's footed pants but can't quite fit my sneakers into the costume, so I take them off and try again, this time in only socks. That proves to be a big mistake, as I'll explain shortly. After that, I slowly slide on the red tube of Bobby's fuselage. Instantly, I am struck by the smell.

In all these years, I have never worn a felt-covered mascot suit— Mr. Met was essentially a hard plastic shell. Felt has a memory, and it's more than happy to reminisce with whomever its occupant might be about all the odors it has picked up over the years. Several years' worth of Max's sweat hits me square in the eyes, which immediately begin to water from the blow.

I almost throw up and very nearly give up right then and there, but thankfully, within moments I myself am sweating and my own musk seems to make the conversation with the scent of mascots past subside to a tolerable level. Without a snug fit in my feet, Bobby's shoes are nearly impossible to control, though, and I walk around as if I have two broken ankles, praying with each step that my own ankles don't take the hint and shatter with a misstep.

We then proceed to make our way to the boardwalk, where we will spend the next hour trying to generate buzz for the upcoming game. The interns are once again armed with free tickets for the event, but we find few takers as most people are headed home for the night, or are at the very tail end of their weekend stay and are just out trying to grab one last breath of that salty sea air before hitting the road.

Max is walking along behind me, and I hear him commenting about how surreal it is to see "me" being "him." I do some of my old tricks, such as "having a conversation with a kid using elaborate but meaningless hand gestures," with all of the blanks being filled in by the child. It's clear that Max is taking copious mental notes.

As expected, most people have no clue who or even what Bobby is, and I am called a lobster, a crab, a Transformer, and a shark—probably the most understandable, given that the red "vertical stabilizer" on my back does resemble a shark's telltale dorsal fin. The confusion is magnified by the fact that the team is two years into a partnership with Reading, the professional soccer team from Holloway's hometown, and has changed the team colors from solid red to Reading's blue-and-white-stripe pattern.

They have also changed the team nickname from the Barons to the Nor'easters. Bobby, though he continues to patrol the boardwalk, is now dubbed Bobby the Storm Chaser. However, the only change in his actual costume is the addition of a Nor'easters jersey, cut to go around the "fin" and carefully safety-pinned to the tube so as not to obscure the sponsorship logo permanently stitched into the back of the costume, the promotional logo of Gillian's Wonderland Pier there for all the world to see, or at least for anyone who approaches the mascot from behind.

I remain out there for close to an hour before we eventually make our way back to the stadium to hide out in the high school until game time, but for some reason on this night—and for the rest of the summer, as fate would have it—there is no air-conditioning. It is an HVAC nightmare that will ultimately postpone the start of the school year due to a mold problem. For me, it's simply one more hurdle to overcome.

While replenishing my fluids, I finally discover the small and almost imperceptible openings in Bobby's feet where my sneakers can slide through and find that with them on, my footing is far less tenuous. The night's trio of referees slowly slip past Bobby's empty shell on their way to get the game started, so I take that as a cue to get back inside the costume.

Next on the agenda is a quiet march to the field, where the sight of Max standing alongside me leads most of the team's employees to wonder who is in the suit if he is not. The players are equally curious when they leave the field following their warmups, headed over to where they stand in line to take part in the ceremonial procession that begins most soccer games.

Immediately, several of the players come over to find out more about my identity, and one whispers to me, "We know it's not Max in there because you're actually good. Maybe you can teach him a thing or two." I can only hope Max is within earshot of that, and that it was said for his benefit and not at his expense.

Once the game starts, I realize that soccer is very different from baseball. For one thing, the running clock and constant flow of action mean that, apart from the few times when an errant kick clears the fence and the teams have to wait for a new ball to be fetched, there are no times when the focus is anywhere but on the field. Essentially, I'm standing around for no good reason, on call just in case somebody happens to score a goal.

Fortunately, goals *are* scored that night, each one punctuated by the same celebratory tune, to which I improvise a dance routine that by the end of the evening would earn me—at least in my mind—a ticket on Mary Murphy's hot tamale train. At the half, the Nor'easters are leading, 2-0.

The attendance for the night is announced at a very generous 481, but after having walked back and forth and interacted with the same six to ten kids for the length of the first half, the whole enterprise is growing a bit tedious. This is especially so because while I am marching up and down on the track that encircles the playing area, the kids are reaching out to me through the fencing that helps prevent them from tumbling out of the bleachers. The restricted access makes it feel more like a prison visit than a sporting event, and it severely limits my ability to truly connect with the fans on a one-to-one level.

The halftime entertainment for this game is far tamer than Friday's mascot invitational. Instead, I am paraded out onto the field of play, where I stand statue still at midfield so that anyone who pays a dollar can throw a Hacky Sack–sized soccer ball at me. The person whose ball lands closest to me wins a free T-shirt for his or her effort.

After more than an hour in the suit, the peppering now over, I finally get to rest for a few seconds in my non-air-conditioned paradise. I throw back a few drinks, and while I wish those drinks were alcoholic in nature in order to dull the pain, they sadly are not—nor could they have been. After all, Ocean City is a dry town.

For a mascot, that's an almost perfect scenario. Regardless of the score of the game, Bobby never has to deal with a disgruntled fan who has had "one too many" and decides to take out his frustrations with the home team's performance by taking a few swings at their very visible representative.

Physically, I am holding up fairly well, but age is certainly catching up with me. My neck is screaming in agony. My shoulders ache. My whole body hates me for deciding to go back out for the second half, but generally speaking the whole experience isn't nearly as bad as I had feared it would be.

Bobby dances three more times this night as the visiting Westchester Flames go down in their nickname by a final score of 5-1. It's the most goals that the Nor'easters have scored at home all season long, a fact I'll happily take some of the credit for. Clearly, my dancing inspired the team to play harder.

Okay, maybe not. But Max is clearly inspired. He's amazed by how much he's learned by watching me. "I can't wait 'til next week's game so I can try out some of the things I saw you doing," he says. That kind of genuine enthusiasm should be contagious, but really, I just want to get into a shower and crawl into my bed and crash.

I was thinking that returning to the suit might help me sufficiently scratch the itch, but this experience is so far removed from what it was like being Mr. Met that the itch continues to rage on (though that may possibly be an allergic reaction to the costume).

Overall, the experience is incredibly positive. The entire Nor'easters organization couldn't have been more supportive, and seeing Max take away so much from watching me perform is certainly rewarding. Still, a soccer game is not a baseball game, full of the rhythms that shaped my development as a mascot performer. This is a totally different experience, and though intuitively I'd known there must be a difference from sport to sport, I don't think I had ever considered just how different they might be.

Maybe that's part of the problem I'm having right now, and as a huge fan of Quentin Tarantino, I've learned that when you've got a problem, there's only one thing you can do to get things handled: You call in the Wolf.

CHAPTER SIX

The Wolf and the Hound

THE DREAM IS ALWAYS THE SAME. It's game day, a half hour or so before kick-off. Like any other Sunday, the pregame schedule has been rehearsed and rehearsed, scripted and timed down to the second. At 11:46:30, Dan Meers knows he is supposed to be on the field for the week's skit. But as he sits half-dressed in his locker room, the music for his routine suddenly begins to play.

What's going on? he thinks. *What time is it?*

Then the realization hits. *I'm supposed to be out there!*

He rushes to get the rest of his costume on before it's too late, but one of his shoes is missing and he can't find it anywhere. Panic sets in. He hears voices asking, "Where is he? Where is the Wolf?"

Meers awakes in a cold sweat, as he slowly catches his breath after once again being haunted by this recurring nightmare.

* * *

THE MAJORITY OF PROMINENT mascots in the world of professional sports come from the world of Major League Baseball. In fact, a 2012 *Forbes* report on a survey done to determine America's favorite sports mascots based on "awareness, likability, and breakthrough (how easily consumers recognize the mascots' affiliation to their teams)" had seven representatives from MLB in its top ten. I'm proud to say that Mr. Met led the pack at No. 1 overall.

The results are not all that surprising. After all, baseball teams play practically every day over a six-month period and there's a rotating pool of fans who buy tickets for one or two of a team's eighty-one home games over the course of a season. Compare that to the NFL, where teams typically play a grand total of ten home games—if you include two preseason dates—and potentially less than that if one of their scheduled home dates is replaced with a trip to London, Mexico City, or Toronto in the league's constant attempts to internationalize the sport.

With season ticket holders filling most, if not all, of the seats in the stadium, exposure to the team's mascot simply doesn't grow over the course of a season. It's the same fans sitting in the same seats, and few, if any, are interested in the sideline shenanigans of what often amounts to a glorified cheerleader with few other game-day duties.

One of the current NFL mascots, who spoke to me on the condition of anonymity, told me that his team was frustrated with the growth of its mascot program. "They constantly tell me that they don't understand why my character is not as well known as [the one from the baseball team in the same city] and don't listen when I tell them that part of the reason is that you have to do more than simply throw me on the field a handful of times a year and expect the public to connect. You have to do appearances. You have to have personal interaction. Right now, we don't have that."

Kansas City does have that in Dan Meers, who has portrayed KC Wolf since the character was "born" in 1990. I caught up with him when he was on a road trip to Fayetteville, Arkansas, where he was scheduled to speak at a church-sponsored basketball banquet. "I may have only a few home dates a year, but I fill up the calendar," Meers says.

Meers worked for a short time as Fredbird, the St. Louis Cardinals' mascot, when he got out of college, but prefers the shorter schedule the NFL has to offer. "It definitely lengthens your career going to football," he jokes. He's certainly proving that to be true, as he still has the ability to suit up more than two decades after he started with the Kansas City Chiefs.

At one time, the team had a man in a Native American headdress ride out onto the field atop a horse named Warpaint, but as public opinion on the appropriateness of the concept changed, the team decided to retire the practice. They ultimately did decide to bring Warpaint the horse back in 2009, though now he is ridden by one of the team's cheerleaders. In the meantime, the Wolf has become an iconic figure in the Kansas City community.

When Meers started out, most teams were using league-sponsored mascots called Huddles, which were tiny little helmeted characters based on each team's nickname. Meers remembers that teams would pay some local kid or intern $50 to come in and wear the suit for the day, but that was it. When the game was over, the costumes got packed back up and shelved until the following home game. Few teams, if any, saw the value in a full-time performer.

That all changed in 1989, when Carl Peterson was brought in as the general manager of the Chiefs. He noticed a group of loyal and very vocal fans that called themselves the Wolfpack, similar to the Cleveland Browns superfans who inhabit the bleachers behind the east end zone at FirstEnergy Stadium, a section better known as the Dawg Pound. "That's where the idea for a Wolf came from," Meers says. "They contacted me in the spring of 1990 to see if I was interested in the job."

Meers had made a name for himself in college mascot competitions, winning the 1989 title for the University of Missouri and finishing second on two other occasions. He had just started working part-time for the Cardinals when the Chiefs asked him to come in for an interview, which clearly ended well for both parties as, to date, it was the last time the team ever had to search for a full-time mascot performer.

"The Chiefs had been so bad for a long, long time and suddenly the team started performing better," Meers says. "They were the hottest ticket in town in the 1990s. They caught fire and made the playoffs, like, eight of my first nine years. So that definitely helped."

It was when he started doing school programs about nutrition, the dangers of drugs, and the importance of reading that his character really began to cement itself as part of the Kansas City community.

"After each school appearance, I'd hand out some promotional pictures of the Wolf," Meers says. "They'd bring them home and put them on their refrigerators or in their rooms, and the parents would see them and start to put two and two together: 'Who is this guy who came to my kid's school? Oh, he's the Chiefs' mascot.' After a few years, everybody in the area—hopefully—knew who KC Wolf was at that point."

Meers has been given an unusual amount of freedom by the Chiefs. He not only does the usual things like birthday parties and corporate events, but is also allowed to be a public speaker and frequently makes appearances as "himself," outside of the Wolf costume. "They trust me to make the right choices. I'm not going to show up at a casino or other places where bad publicity might result," Meers tells me in his deep, soothing baritone voice. "What some people don't know about me is that I am actually an ordained Baptist minister. That's where my passion is—with my faith and with my family."

While Meers considers himself to be relaxed and easygoing outside of the suit, a different personality has been known, from time to time, to come out of him when he gets in costume. This "tough guy" made his first appearance during the Pro Bowl in Hawaii, in front of the best players in the league.

"It was 2001," Meers says. "This guy comes running onto the field with his shirt off and the security guys are trying to chase him down, and of course he's a lot quicker than these big old Hawaiian dudes. The next thing you know, this guy just kind of runs over in my direction. And I thought, *Well, I can take this guy down.* Drunk guys aren't that hard to tackle. So [when] he got close, I jumped on him and took him down and the crowd went nuts. And the best part is at that point, the big security guys are right there to get him, so I don't have to worry about the guy hauling off and punching me."

At the airport the following day, Meers bought the local paper to read on the eight-hour flight back home and was stunned to see the following on the front page of the *Honolulu Star-Bulletin*: "The best, most entertaining tackle of yesterday's Pro Bowl at Aloha Stadium was not delivered by Ray Lewis of the Baltimore Ravens or Junior Seau of the San Diego Chargers. It was applied by Dan Meers of the Kansas City Chiefs." Naturally, before boarding the plane, Meers went back and bought several more copies of the paper to give out to friends and family back home.

The next time it happened, Meers didn't have to worry about buying any out-of-town newspapers. The *Kansas City Star* took care of spreading the word that KC Wolf had once again played a role in subduing a fan who ended up where he was not supposed to be—this time during the team's 2007 home opener versus the Minnesota Vikings. At the time, the Chiefs had not made the playoffs in twelve years, and ultimately the team would end up losing the last nine games of the season to finish at 4-12. But on that Sunday, perhaps inspired by the Wolf, the Chiefs were victorious, 13-10. "When the sports radio guys are saying the most entertaining thing that happened at the game is the mascot tackling a drunk, you know something's wrong," Meers laments. "But I have a lot of people still talking to me about that tackle."

Meers, who has logged more than thirty thousand miles on his stationary bicycle over the years to help him stay in shape, has begun the transition to life after football. He has hired a backup performer to help with the huge number of requests for outside appearances that flood the team's e-mail inbox. He says he finds it hard to watch somebody else be KC Wolf and that at first, it drove him a little nuts.

"It's very tricky," Meers says. "I've learned to see someone else be KC Wolf. The first couple of times, it just drove me crazy to sit and watch somebody else in the costume because you develop a character for fifteen years or more and you become very picky about his mannerisms and everything like that. I've tried to learn to loosen up a little bit, but I've also done a lot of coaching over the years. The more [my backup] watches me, the more of my mannerisms he picks up. It's a process for both of us."

Still, as long as they keep making ibuprofen, Meers has no plans to quit anytime soon. "Mascots help remind us that you should not take life too seriously," he says. "With all the other stuff that comes along in life—and there's plenty of stuff, both good and bad—you've got to remember that the sun is going to come up again tomorrow and God is still good, and we will get through it. Heck, laughter is like changing a baby's diaper. It doesn't change anything permanently, but it sure makes things more bearable for a while."

● ● ●

THE SUN ALMOST DIDN'T COME UP FOR GLENN STREET in December of 2012, however. He needed open-heart surgery to become "bionic" by having a mechanical valve installed to keep his ticker ticking. Fortunately all went well and his friends—of whom there are many—breathed a big sigh of relief. By early January of 2013, Street was already walking up to two miles a day, and while he spent a lot of time sleeping to recover, it was clear that the worst was behind him.

Ironically, it was a heart problem that originally led Street down the path to a career as one of Canada's most beloved mascots, Harvey the Hound, probably the most recognizable figure in the extended family of the NHL's Calgary Flames.

In the early 1980s, Street was working as a volunteer for the promotions committee for the annual Calgary Stampede, a huge, ten-day event featuring a rodeo and concerts that is to the Canadian city what Mardi Gras is to New Orleans. Street was offered a chance to attend the Grey Cup—the Canadian Football League's Super Bowl—all expenses paid, provided, of course, he was willing to wear the mascot costume for the Stampede. Street was confused, because a co-worker named John was the one who tended to exclusively don the Harry the Horse costume.

"They told me there was a problem with John," Street recounts. "The costume weighs so much, about 85 pounds. So, John's in the hospital. What they figure happened is that the weight of the costume compressed his rib cage and one of his ribs is pressing against his heart." John needed to get that rib removed, so Street took his place.

That's when Street ended up meeting Grant Kelba, who at the time was doing a character for Calgary's CFL team, the Stampeders. Kelba had pitched the idea of a new mascot character to the NHL's Calgary Flames, which had recently relocated to the city from Atlanta. The Flames loved the concept and Harvey the Hound was about to become a reality. The only problem was that Kelba was too busy to handle the performing duties for two teams on his own. So he offered Street a chance to be a partner in the enterprise.

Interestingly enough, Kelba and Street owned the Hound costume, so for the first few seasons the Flames were, in essence, renting their mascot on a per-game basis, much in the same way the team would hire an organist to play for the crowd. "They wanted to do it that way because if it didn't work, they wanted to be able to say, 'No, that's not our mascot. We just hire these two schmucks to come in and wear the costume for us,'" Street says. What happened, though, was the opposite. "The character became so popular and so closely tied to the team that they eventually came back to us and said they cannot afford *not* to have ownership of Harvey. So they cut a deal with us, and now they do, in fact, own the character."

Harvey the Hound was the first NHL mascot, so Street certainly had no idea this was what he was going to end up doing for a living long-term. "I don't know if I was ever clear on what I would do when I grew up," he says. "I never sat down and said, 'I'm going to be a professional mascot.' They were still very new. The Chicken broke open the field for everybody, and the CFL had a few mascots, but none with very strong personalities."

Street is a native Calgarian, which he says is actually quite unusual. "Calgary has always been one of the fastest-growing cities in North America, so when I graduated from high school, most of my classmates had moved *to* Calgary from somewhere else. Very few were from here originally." Most kids there grow up playing hockey or skiing, and since Street's family had a mountain cabin, he spent far more time on the slopes than on the ice. As it turns out, as Harvey, he didn't have to spend much time on the ice either.

"Hockey mascots really know how to work the crowd because they spend the entire game immersed in the stands," Street says. "They don't have a dugout they can stand on. They simply move about the arena interacting with the fans. In baseball, you get to go on the field. In basketball, you get to do all that gymnastics stuff. Not so in hockey."

The other thing that makes hockey unique is the speed of the game itself. "There's no downtime in hockey. It's a pretty fast-moving sport," Street says. "You can go to a baseball game and sit there eating nachos and drinking beer and then you hear the crack of the bat and you know to look up. In hockey, you pretty much have to watch [the game action] all the time because if something happens, you're likely to miss it unless you're paying attention."

Street adds, though, that a lot has changed since he left the job shortly after the Flames bought the character. (Street went on to build his own company, Street Characters, which has created mascots for more than thirty teams in the four major sports, including Blitz of the Seattle Seahawks, Bernie of the Colorado Avalanche, and Southpaw of the Chicago White Sox, as well as countless others for universities and corporations all over North America. Grant Kelba continued to perform as Harvey until he retired in 1999.)

"Back then, there were only three or four announcements during the course of the game itself," Street says. "Technology wasn't where it is today. So during the breaks, the whistle would blow and everyone in the crowd would start looking for Harvey to see what was going to happen. Now, with video scoreboards and sponsorship obligations and all of these other things, the games are much more scripted than they used to be. So today it is actually more difficult for Harvey at a Flames game, because he gets only three or four time slots, rather than the other way around."

Street believes that mascots are often so popular because even people who might not be fans of the sport can appreciate them and what they do and the enjoyment they bring to the game experience. "Not everybody who goes to a game is a fan. But everybody is there to have a good time," Street says. "Nobody wants to be miserable. So mascots are able to be a fun diversion for those people who aren't diehards." Even in hockey-mad Calgary, Street believes, if you sent Harvey walking around the city next to the marquee player on the team, more people would recognize Harvey, even if the player was wearing his jersey.

Of course, fans of other teams recognize Harvey as well. The Hound has frequently been subjected to verbal and physical attacks from the supporters of other hockey teams, specifically those of the rival Edmonton Oilers. Street firmly believes that the reason Edmonton is one of only four NHL teams *without* a mascot (the Dallas Stars,

New York Rangers, and Philadelphia Flyers being the others) is simply because Calgary has one. That's how fierce the rivalry between the teams is.

Street recalls once being escorted out of Northlands Coliseum in Edmonton during a playoff game, after defenseman Steve Smith of the Oilers scored an "own goal" by accidentally shooting the puck off of his own goalie's leg and into the net, allowing Calgary to take the lead. "Security came up to me and said I needed to go for my own safety," Street says. "I think they were right. People were not in a real friendly or happy mood."

Still, as well known as Harvey the Hound is north of the border, not a ton of people in the United States had any idea who he was until January of 2003. That weekend, Street was on vacation at a bed and breakfast in the Rocky Mountain foothills, out in the middle of nowhere, watching the Flames and Oilers game on television.

At one point, Harvey was straddling the Plexiglas that surrounds the rink. He was busy exhorting the fans to cheer louder and louder, and as the Flames were winning 4-0 at the time, they were more than happy to oblige. Harvey then got back on the crowd's side of the glass and ended up walking past the Oilers' bench. In so doing, he unexpectedly found himself leaning over in front of then–Oilers head coach Craig MacTavish.

Now, one of the identifying features of Harvey's costume is his red tongue, quite a bit of which hangs outside his open mouth. So, when Harvey leaned over, the tongue was dangling directly in front of MacTavish, who decided to reach up and give it a yank. "What was really interesting about that entire incident was, first of all, I loved MacTavish's response, which was just giving the tongue a playful tug," Street says. "And when [the tongue] came off, you can tell he froze and was like 'Oh, no,' and then sort of a fraction of a second later he sort of realizes what he's done in the home team's building and then he panics and he's looking around and he throws it into the crowd."

As it turns out, the incident seemed to invigorate the Oilers, who went on to score the next three goals, cutting the Flames' lead to 4-3. After the game, the incident was all reporters wanted to talk about. But all MacTavish said was "I just checked my job description and it doesn't say anything about Harvey the Hound in there."

What Street still wonders about to this day is why, shortly after the incident happened, the owner of the B&B told him he had a phone call. "It was Toronto Maple Leafs television looking for a comment from me about the incident. I still have no idea how they found me. Nobody knew where I was."

Street does use the Tongue Incident as a cautionary tale illustrating that mascots need to be careful not to do anything that is going to have a direct effect on the outcome of the game, either intentionally or unintentionally. But sometimes, as in this case, it's unavoidable. "Characters are all about entertainment, so if it creates buzz and people end up laughing, in the end, it's a good thing," he says. "I mean, it's not like he slugged MacTavish."

And so, there's no need for Harvey to have any regrets in this instance. But Street does have one regret of his own. "The repair bill to reattach the tongue was $1.96. I should have sent it to MacTavish," he chuckles.

* * *

MEERS AND STREET BOTH AGREE that mascot performers need to always remember that all eyes are on them, inside the costume and out. You never know who might be watching, so it's essential to be on your best behavior regardless of whether you're working for a major league team or at the local car wash.

Meers says his travels used to cause him to frequently drive past a local business that had an animal as its car wash mascot. He'd be tasked to stand out at the side of the busy road and wave at cars to entice them to stop in and take advantage of the services being offered. "The first couple of times I saw this mascot, I was so impressed," Meers says. "I mean, he was energetic, he was waving to the cars that went by, really high energy, and maybe the first few times I saw him I thought, *Man, that guy's got potential.*"

Meers has had to work street corners for grand openings himself, so he knows it's a thankless job. However, it is in fact a job—and as such, one expects a certain level of performance. Even from a guy in an animal suit.

"Then, all of a sudden, the next couple times I go by, I notice he's got, like, a bench sitting out there and he's just kind of resting there," Meers says. "Talk about going downhill in a hurry. The last time I saw him, he had his phone in his hand—his actual hand, not even his paw—and was texting away. I honked my horn and he didn't even look up. That guy was a disgrace to mascots."

Street says it's crucial for a professional mascot performer to stay on the straight and narrow outside of the costume as well. "If a mascot is involved in a domestic dispute or arrested for driving under the influence, it makes the papers just as it would for any player," Street warns. "So it's really important for the performer to understand that even outside of the costume, they're under public scrutiny. They've got to remember that. I've seen a lot of performers get in trouble because their ego is bigger than their costume. They do something they shouldn't have and they quickly find out they no longer have a job."

CHAPTER SEVEN

Really, Really Big Man on Campus

IMAGINE YOU'RE A FRESHMAN entering your second semester at one of the most prestigious universities in the United States. You're no longer feeling as lost as you did when you left your childhood home in September and ventured out on your own for the very first time. Over the past few months those initial nerves have slowly vanished and the campus, which once seemed overwhelmingly large and frightening to you, has become your new home. You feel perfectly safe here, until ...

Walking out into the main plaza area one day, you hear screams. Amid the confusion and chaos, you try to locate the source of the mayhem and then stare in horror as your eyes finally focus on a fellow student who is under attack. His clothes have been ripped off and a gang of assailants is pummeling him with a steady supply of fluorescent light bulbs, the elongated tubes shattering as they make contact with his bare skin, leaving the victim bruised and bloodied.

Why is nobody coming to this poor soul's aid? Hang on a second. Why is everybody laughing and bursting into applause? What the hell is going on here?

This was the scene that Jonathan Strange stumbled across while walking to class as a Stanford freshman in 2008. At most schools, such an incident would likely result in police involvement, suspensions for those involved, and perhaps even jail time. But, being as it's February in Palo Alto, California, incidents like this are par for the course. In fact, the victim had orchestrated the entire onslaught himself. Why would anyone volunteer for such abuse? It's simple. He was auditioning to become the school mascot.

Tree Week, as it is known, is a cross between fraternity hazing and the Hunger Games. Although Stanford University has no official mascot—its athletic teams are known as the Cardinal, a reference to the school color—the Tree has been accepted by the administration as the unofficial mascot.

Until 1972, the school's athletic teams had used the nickname Indians, but they discontinued the offensive moniker after protests from Native American groups. While it's fairly difficult to create a character using only a color as inspiration, the appearance of a redwood on the school seal along with its use on the official logo of the city of Palo Alto makes the leap to a costumed tree seem much less random.

In 1975, the school's marching band put on a halftime show to "propose" potential new mascots for the university. Although intended to be a joke—other options included the French Fry and the Steaming Manhole—the Tree actually started to develop a bit of a cult following. Over time, the role of Tree became part of the accepted culture on campus, and the band continues to select the person upon whom the honor of being the Tree is bestowed.

Jonathan Strange grew up in the San Mateo area, just ten miles away from the Stanford campus. "I had been to a lot of baseball games when I was little. The band doesn't normally play at the baseball games, but I'd also been to a couple of football games and the Tree was always there." Growing up, he had noticed that each year the costume was different—some better, some worse—but didn't know much about the history of the mascot.

After witnessing the light bulb incident and finding out what was really behind it, a light bulb went off above his head. He knew he had to be the Tree. Strange did his research so that when the next year's competition came around, he would be ready to hit the ground running.

Although it's not as secretive as, say, Yale's Skull and Bones, Strange didn't want to reveal all of the hurdles potential candidates have to jump through. What he was willing to share was that typically there's an informational meeting that is open to the entire student body, where anybody can go and learn more about the audition process. A lot of mundane details are shared, like, for example, the schedule for future interviews with band management and former Trees, as well as the reading of the rules and regulations.

However, what most people don't know heading into this meeting is that the audition process has already begun. In order to become the Tree, you have to "prove yourself worthy of the honor" by performing a series of outlandish stunts. Some stunts in the past did not work out so well. Reportedly, one student got shot and another was set on fire. Another dressed up as a deer and launched himself in front of the university president's car.

As a result of past misfortune, the current stunt restrictions state "no fire, no electrocution, no serious bodily harm that would result in a trip to the hospital—even if the candidate chooses not to go—and nothing illegal." The bodily harm clause is what eliminated our intrepid incandescent piñata from the competition in *his* ill-fated attempt at fame.

But prior winners have managed to win the favor of the judging committee by eating live snakes, "branding" themselves with the shape of a tree using leeches, and skydiving naked into Stanford Stadium during a game. That said, if a stunt "works," even one that breaks the rules might not result in disqualification. One recent winner impressed the panel by dressing up in a duck costume (one of the school's conference rivals is the Oregon Ducks) and allowing them to take turns using a stun gun on him.

In order for a stunt to be "official," it has to be witnessed by the outgoing Tree, whose gig runs for one year and one year only. So, if you're serious about winning, you have to do your homework, coordinating with the current Tree in advance and making sure that he knows when and where your next stunt will be.

"From the initial meeting, there's like a week and a half or so before they name the new Tree," Strange says. "You will keep getting invites back for interviews as long as you remain a candidate in their eyes by performing stunts."

The best way to make a huge first impression is to arrive at the informational meeting in grand style. The selection committee may not know who you are before you show up, but when you recruit a bunch of your friends to dress up as reindeer and ride bicycles into the meeting while you dress up in a Santa Claus suit and get dragged behind them on a sleigh, they certainly will have their curiosity piqued.

Strange actually fell off the sleigh during the stunt, but had prepared a "part two" to his entrance. "I ripped off the Santa suit, and I'm wearing a tuxedo made out of duct tape," he said. "I shouted, 'I'm tired of being Santa. I'm ready to be the fucking Tree!'"

With only three other students making a similar kind of splash, including one candidate who constructed a fiberglass rocket-man helmet and arrived via zip line, in practical terms, the field for the 2009–2010 Tree was set before the meeting was adjourned.

According to Strange, the only people who really know what the committee is looking for in any given year are the members of the committee themselves. "You have to be yourself and hope your personality fits. Sometimes people try out three or four times and don't get it because they're trying to guess what the selection group is looking for," he says. "If you're a completely different person from one year to the next, it comes off sort of weird."

Being himself, by the time Strange welded himself into a four-foot-diameter round steel cage and had his friends propel his prison toward a bunch of empty beer kegs in an impromptu session of bowling on the quad, victory was all but certain. Strange had achieved his goal, but the hard work was just getting started.

❋ ❋ ❋

THE AUDITION PROCESS AT MOST SCHOOLS is a little more traditional than the one at Stanford, and the perks that go along with the prize can vary greatly from campus to campus.

At St. Joseph's University in Philadelphia, the mascot gets a full scholarship, though this is not the norm by any means. The student who is tasked with being the Hawk has to earn that free ride by serving the first season as team manager for the men's basketball team before donning the suit in the next season. No, there's no laundry detail involved with that, but the ability to order twenty pizzas and multiple sandwiches from a local eatery for a postgame meal is certainly going to hasten your acceptance in the locker room.

The Hawk travels to every single game the St. Joseph's basketball team plays, and from the moment it hits the court until the final buzzer of the contest, its arms are in constant motion, flapping up and down without stopping—a living embodiment of the motto The Hawk Will Never Die! As exhausting as it is to watch, I can't imagine the physical toll such a tradition takes on the performer.

The name of the person in the costume is far from a secret. For the 2012–2013 school year, the Hawk costume was ably filled by Ian Klinger. He says the selection process was more like a real-world job interview than a demonstration of his athletic prowess. In fact, not once did he even have to put on the costume. They simply asked him if he thought he'd be able to handle the physical demands and he told them that, given his track background, he thought he could.

"I had to submit a résumé and a letter stating why I wanted to be the Hawk," Klinger said. "I also needed to have a letter of recommendation from a faculty member. Then I went through a series of three interviews, the last one being with [men's basketball head coach Phil] Martelli." Klinger says Martelli was looking for a well-rounded, trustworthy individual to join the basketball "family." After all, what happens at practice is supposed to stay at practice.

As for the constant arm flapping, Klinger says he originally underestimated how much of a physical strain it would be. However, as he got more and more games under his belt, he soon "grew so used to it" that now he's not even consciously aware that he's doing it.

Klinger considers being the Hawk such an honor that he'd have signed up to do it even if a scholarship wasn't attached. "I got to travel all year with an NCAA Division I basketball team," he says. "I've gotten invited to show up at numerous weddings and had the opportunity to do so much community service. It has all just been incredible. The scholarship is just a bonus."

While Klinger's identity is something that St. Joseph's happily promotes in order to showcase one of the student body's most positive role models, some schools are loath to let the cat out of the bag. In fact, at Michigan State University, keeping confidential the identity of Sparty—a muscular, green ancient warrior—is a requirement of the job.

Should the name of the student inside the costume be disclosed, he or she is immediately removed from the position. Yes, a few trusted confidants are allowed to be in on the secret, as it would be impossible for any Sparty to explain away his or her frequent disappearances without some close friends getting suspicious. Still, the school is looking for a performer who is willing to remain humble until after graduation and put Sparty's interests ahead of his or her own.

It is certainly understandable why a school might want to ensure that the student inside what often amounts to the most visible icon of the institution is not going to embarrass or otherwise tarnish the college's image. In today's world of social media and the Internet, it doesn't take long for a poorly thought-out picture to be uploaded to Facebook or for a YouTube video to go viral and have the national media talking about a university for all the wrong reasons.

That's what happened when West Virginia student Jonathan Kimble proudly posted photographs and a video of a December 2012 hunting trip in which he used a rifle to shoot a bear out of a tree. Although there was nothing illegal about it, the fact that Kimble's rifle was part of his Mountaineer mascot costume—one of the few "characters" that takes human form—many people found the incident disturbing and offensive.

A spokesman for the school said there was nothing that prohibited Kimble from using the weapon during a legal hunting trip, and although an agreement was reached that the senior would no longer use the rifle in such a capacity, the school nevertheless took a public relations hit from the incident that it might not have had Kimble been more anonymous.

Of course, the fact that the West Virginia Mountaineer is very visibly Kimble in a coonskin cap did not help matters in this case. If the school's mascot performer wore a more traditional oversize character suit, recognition might not have occurred as quickly, if at all.

* * *

AT MY ALMA MATER, SYRACUSE UNIVERSITY, the school mascot has taken various forms throughout the years. In the 1920s, the mascot was a live animal—Vita the Goat. However, eventually it was replaced by the Saltine Warrior, born of a hoax perpetrated by the student newspaper that claimed that the remains of a sixteenth-century Onondagan chief had been unearthed during the expansion of the campus.

A student dressed up as an Indian accompanied Syracuse sports teams onto the field until 1978, when a real Onondagan chief, Oren Lyons—who had once starred on the school's lacrosse team—led a protest to encourage a move to a less offensive mascot. Failed efforts in establishing a permanent character in succeeding years included a Roman gladiator, an orange Superman clone, and Egnaro the Troll.

After the opening of the Carrier Dome in 1980 and well into the mid-1990s, it wasn't unusual to see several mascots in various sections of the stadium attempting to cheer the 'Cuse to victory. There was the Dome Ranger, a masked cowboy whom television cameras often caught running from under one basket to the other in an effort to whip the crowd into a frenzy. There was Dome Eddie, who sported a giant orange wig and could have been a distant cousin of Rollen Stewart, who became famous for his rainbow wig and the "John 3:16" signs he held up at sporting events all over the country.

For every Dome Dog and Dome Knitter that sprang up, there were countless other attempts to win fan affection that came and went without notice. At one point, the building's head of security, Gene Haumann, unintentionally became a mascot. Traditionally, it was Haumann who would deliver the halftime statistics to the media seated courtside shortly after the start of the second half. Emerging from the tunnel, stack of papers in hand, Haumann was hard to miss.

Not only was Haumann sturdy of frame, his brightly colored sports jacket and white handlebar mustache also had a way of catching one's eye as he made his stroll around the basketball court. The student section certainly took notice, and started serenading Haumann with a chant of "Dome Guy" that began when he emerged from the tunnel and continued in a rhythmic pattern until his tour of the press tables was complete and he returned from whence he came.

As the Dome Guy chant echoed down on Haumann during one key Big East contest versus hated Georgetown in March of 1991, the Syracuse basketball team went on a huge run to start the second half after the visiting Hoyas had gone into halftime with the lead. When the Hoyas called a time-out to try and regroup, Haumann decided to make a second tour of his route so as not to jinx the good fortune. The Orange crowd went, for lack of a better term, bananas, and the energy in the building helped buoy the team to victory.

Haumann, alas, ended up retiring a few short seasons later, and sadly, the chant left with him.

Throughout it all, though, there has been the Orange, who first appeared in the early 1980s and finally was recognized by the university as their official mascot in 1995, after a brief flirtation with changing the team nickname to the Wolves was voted down by the student body at large. Otto, a nickname for the Orange that had been adopted by the cheerleading squad for its alliterative allure, was also embraced by the school as the official moniker for the lovable citrus-inspired character.

* * *

IN 2010, NICK NATARIO WAS AT A CROSSROADS. Ever since middle school, he had wanted to go into journalism to be a reporter. When he visited Syracuse University in 2003 on the same day the men's basketball team won their first NCAA championship, the atmosphere all over campus made it impossible for him not to get swept up in the excitement. Although he ended up applying to a bunch of other schools just to be safe, there was no doubt in Natario's mind where he would ultimately end up. When Syracuse said yes to him—early decision, no less—he accepted on the spot.

Like many broadcasting hopefuls who arrive on campus hoping to become the next Bob Costas, Mike Tirico, or Sean McDonough, Natario started working at WAER, the student radio station that does play-by-play of men's athletics, during his freshman year. However, fate had a different path for Natario to follow.

Knowing about his love of sports and that Natario had once held a summer job as a costumed character at Six Flags New England, Nick's resident advisor showed him an ad in the student paper for the upcoming Otto tryouts.

"I had no desire to be Otto. I never played my high school mascot. I never did any sports mascotting," Natario told me. "I already had a lot of activities on my plate, but I'm someone who likes to keep myself busy. So I went, just to see what this had to offer."

So what goes on during a more traditional mascot audition at the university level? Unlike at a certain Northern California school, the process is pretty mundane. "The first day we got there, about fourteen people showed up," Natario said. "There was a group interview where we asked any questions we might have had about the process and then we each had to find an ordinary object somewhere in the building and do some improvisation—do three things with our item that it's not supposed to be used for."

After that, each auditioning student got to get inside the Otto costume and follow simple commands such as "blowing a kiss," the trick being that the performer inside the suit had to remember that Otto's mouth is located at the level of an average person's crotch. Once everybody had their turn inside the Orange, the field was whittled down to the final four candidates for two open spots.

Natario, who made the cut, had one week to come up with a

ninety-second skit featuring music and props. With a background in band, Natario decided to bring a drum with him and used his percussive prowess to help wow the judges. "It was pretty basic stuff, and looking back now, if I did something like that at a professional audition, I would not get the job," Natario said. "But back then, it must have been enough."

Natario enjoyed his time as Otto, flying all over the country with the football team, appearing on *Wheel of Fortune,* filming nationally televised commercials, getting swag from Nike, and having his own personal trainer from the athletic department to help him keep in game shape. Unfortunately, that training couldn't help Natario when he fell from atop a cheerleading pyramid and injured his knee in the fall of 2007.

Fearful that his senior year might be ruined, Natario endured the pain and kept mum about how badly he was hurt. Natario had aspirations of becoming a professional mascot after meeting some peers at national mascot competitions who were already working as part-time backups in the NBA. Their encouragement helped Natario come to the realization that he was quite good at this mascotting business. In fact, his strong showing at the Universal Cheerleaders Association national championship led to a feature article in the Syracuse *Post-Standard.*

As fate would have it, the same reporter interviewed Dave Raymond shortly after talking to Natario. Raymond asked the reporter for Natario's contact information and eventually offered him a job with his company. Natario thought it was a great opportunity to work with one of the best in the business and hoped that, through Raymond's connections, he'd eventually be able to make a move to MLB or the NBA.

Natario's job was to tour the country, performing at minor league stadiums alongside Reggie the Purple Party Dude, a character

Raymond had created in 2001. However, the toll exacted by red-eye flights and limited sleep and the discovery that he had been dealing with a torn meniscus since his pyramid accident all brought the recent graduate to a tipping point.

"I wanted to be major league," Natario said. "That's what I wanted to do. I heard there was an opening with the Tampa Bay Rays and I wanted the experience of auditioning for a professional team. I wasn't even sure if I wanted the job, but I got a phone call from Tampa and they were like, 'We'd like you to come down,' and I was shocked, because I finally heard something from someone. I thought, *Wow, I might be actually good enough to get a pro job.*"

Unfortunately, being young, Natario decided to keep the fact that he was planning to audition to himself. As a result, he says, he feared that if he went to Tampa Bay, there was a chance he could lose his job. Natario decided to go through with the audition anyway.

When he arrived in Tampa, he discovered that he was one of six candidates for the position. It was an incredibly hot day, and each potential mascot had to perform a "grand entrance," a comedic skit, some improv with props, an impromptu baseball game with some kids recruited for the tryout, and finally, a four-minute dance routine.

Natario's inexperience may have been his undoing. "I didn't take a break, even though they said 'If you need a breather you can take one.' I was like, 'Screw that! I exercise like crazy, I can do it,' and so I didn't. I was so winded by the time that dance came on that I could barely move. I was dying."

Also dying were his chances at getting the job, as the ultimate winner of the coveted prize was a performer who had taken three breaks during his audition and, as a result, knocked the dance portion out of the park. When Natario got the rejection call from the

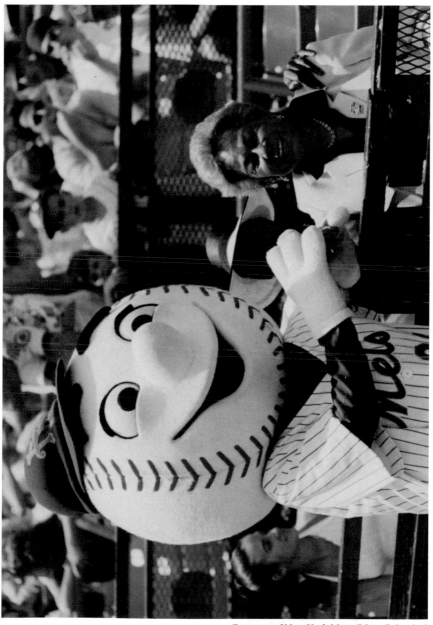

Rachel Robinson gets her picture taken with a well-behaved Mr. Met.

Courtesy of the author

Mr. Met always wants to be the center of attention.

It's Yankee fan Mayor
Rudy Giuliani's
worst nightmare.

Courtesy of the author

Courtesy of AP Images

Max Patkin, the Clown Prince of Baseball—it all started with him.

The Chicken, feeling a little peckish?

The Phanatic proclaims his innocence.

We're ready for our close-up at the Vet for the 1997 All-Star Game.

The "old" Mr. Met costume visits Pittsburgh, circa 1994.

Courtesy of the author

The "mascots" prepare for the halftime steeplechase.

Courtesy of the author

Max Woerner is beside himself with excitement.

My comeback begins.

Bobby in action on the Ocean City boardwalk.

KC Wolf cheers on the Chiefs.

Harvey the Hound makes an appearance, complete with tongue.

Jonathan Strange offers his interpretation of Stanford's Tree.

There's no place like Dome for Otto the Orange.

Inside Buster's Lakewood lair.

Early action from my farewell performance.

Billy the Marlin
always looks sharp.

Stomper tosses out
a souvenir.

David Raymond lends a hand at his Mascot Boot Camp.

The mascot menagerie learns to shake and shimmy.

Courtesy of Getty Images

The Gorilla takes
the profession
to new heights.

Courtesy of the author

My son, Xander, at Halloween.
The apple doesn't fall far from the tree.

Rays, they told him that he was clearly very good in the costume and that he could probably do a very good job on the marketing side of things, but they were really looking for someone with more contemporary dance moves, which was what ultimately tipped the scales in the other candidate's favor.

To add insult to injury, the candidate they hired actually used to work under Natario at Raymond Entertainment. Shortly thereafter, Natario's fears came to fruition as he indeed found himself out of a job. The decision to go to Tampa may not have been the only factor in his dismissal, but it certainly couldn't have helped. Though disappointed with how it all turned out, Natario still thinks highly of Raymond. "He's a great person," Natario said. "I don't regret having worked with him at all. I learned so much. That's why I wanted the job with him because I feel, before working with Dave, if I had gotten a professional job I would have failed because I didn't know how to sustain a program. Now, I don't think I would be perfect at it, but I know I would be a lot better."

Sounding bitter and defeated and with his wounds still very fresh, Natario was pondering his next move. "I guess I'm going to try out for the Connecticut Sun in the WNBA," he said. "I mean, I recently put together a résumé tape for broadcasting and started applying for reporting jobs. I'm done with this whole mascot thing. But the market is so tough right now. I don't know. I could do the WNBA. The Sun are having an open casting call. Who does that? What kind of good performers do you think you're going to find doing that?"

With his family very anti-mascot and hoping to see Nick one day sitting at the anchor desk on the *NBC Nightly News*, the pressure to move on is huge. Plus, Natario's biggest fear in looking into the future is seeing himself in his thirties, suiting up in some lame costume at a theme park just to make enough money to pay his rent.

"Eventually I do want to get married and have kids just like everybody else, and I want the stability factor," Natario said. "How long do I have to wait for a gig to come around? How long *can* I wait?"

* * *

"I CAN'T WAIT," SAYS JONATHAN STRANGE when I catch up with him. He's already looking forward to the next Tree tryouts, when he will be the judge, jury, and executioner. "I mean, I do like a lot of attention, because I feel I deserve attention. You do get a mini God complex that comes with Tree. I mean, you are, like, the king of the school. I just feel there aren't going to be any other people who are better deserving of being Tree than I am."

Strange removed all doubt that his stunts were a cut above the rest when he cemented his selection, quite literally, by staging a mock Mafia kidnapping of himself. His friends, dressed in pinstripe suits and dark sunglasses, abducted him and shoved his feet into buckets of cement—he wore boots to prevent chemical burns—and then they tossed him into a nearby lake.

Once his victory became official, Strange spent the summer creating his own costume using the small budget given to him by the band. In the past, there have been pine trees and palm trees, trees with traditional green-hued foliage and those who went with Cardinal-colored leaves. Strange chose to weld together a frame that he could easily collapse in order to carry it onto planes. His leaves are shiny and silver, with a second set of leaves in pink that he can swap out in order to promote breast cancer awareness during the month of October.

Part of that budget also has to go for the hiring of "Tree protection services" in the form of bodyguards, who prevent any fans from hassling Strange when he's mingling with the public. It's not hard to

imagine that Strange might push a few buttons of opposing supporters when he says things like "I hate USC and Cal equally. Some people
say they're just bitter Stanford rejects. I love to beat them both, but
let's face it: It's not always possible to win when your football team
has a GPA of 3.5 and we're facing a team with a GPA of under 2.0."

Strange believes he is simply being himself. "I'm not playing a
tree character. I'm just me, wearing a tree costume," he says. "But
they chose me for a reason, and I'm the best person to fill the job. You
just can't have any shame. I'm badass. If we win, great. But if we lose,
oh well. . . . 'Hey, that guy is dancing like a crazy little motherfucker
and having fun.' We have a lot of fun here. It's not whether you win or
lose, it's being in an awesome place like Stanford."

Kids say the darndest things, don't they?

CHAPTER EIGHT

We Have Such Sights to Show You

AS WE FINISH WALKING through a maze of corridors, we stand before the door. After slowly turning the knob in the cramped quarters, the dark, windowless room begins to reveal itself to us. Once our eyes grow accustomed to the dim light the opened door lets in, we gasp in horror as we see a trio of lifeless bodies, heads and limbs removed, hanging from chains holding them securely to the ceiling of their previously undisturbed tomb.

Perhaps taking the night of August 21, 2012, to Clive Barker levels of terror is a bit much, but the truth is that equal parts excitement and fear do course through my body as I venture to Lakewood, New Jersey, to once again fill the fur and partake in the next leg of my mascot journey.

Lakewood is home to the Class A minor league affiliate of the Philadelphia Phillies, nicknamed the BlueClaws. Lakewood is also home to a huge Orthodox Jewish population as well as Beth Medrash Govoha, the largest yeshiva in North America, so naturally the choice of shellfish as a team mascot makes little to no sense. However, when you hold a name-the-team contest and more of the five thousand entries read "BlueClaws" than any other moniker, so let it be written, so let it be done.

For those of you unfamiliar with the hierarchy of baseball leagues, affiliated minor leagues serve as pipelines to the majors, providing young players with the opportunity to work their way up the ladder toward the goal of making a major league roster. The Triple-A level is the step just below the big leagues and is populated primarily by prospects on the cusp of getting their first taste of "the Show" and demoted veterans hoping to play their way back to the game's highest level. Below that, there is Double-A, then three levels of Class A ball, followed by Rookie.

The players at Lakewood, for the most part, have survived their first year as professional athletes and earned promotions to Class A. They'll be asked to play a 140-game schedule over a six-month span in order to see how they cope with the demands of a long season. Those who impress their organizations at this level will either get promotions to Class A Advanced or perhaps even to Double-A the following season—one step closer to their dream.

Those who struggle will be left behind or perhaps not be asked back at all, their careers ending before they even have a chance to begin. It's a stressful environment to be sure, but having made it this far, optimism is the primary feeling in the clubhouse, as opposed to the desperation that permeates some of the higher levels, where more and more players come to the realization that their reach outdistances their grasp.

The atmosphere is especially charged in the BlueClaws clubhouse because only about a month earlier, they had been visited by an alum of the team who brought with him a real-life success story for them to latch on to. Ryan Howard, the 2005 National League Rookie of the Year and 2006 NL Most Valuable Player, had been sitting right there alongside these baseball neophytes as he played three games at FirstEnergy Park in order to rehab an injured Achilles tendon. Big league teams will often send their stars to whatever location makes the most sense for them geographically, regardless of the level of competition, just to get them some game action on their road to recovery.

Howard had played for the BlueClaws in 2002, and his retired No. 29 jersey is displayed proudly on the outfield wall, just right of advertisements for not one, but two local IHOPs. He is living proof of the attainability of the goal that each one of these players has set for himself, and nearly a month after his visit, the effects of his short time in the dugout are still quite evident. Howard went 5-for-8 with four RBIs in his three-game stint, and the fans came out in full force to see him in action. The crowd nearly doubled in size to eight thousand cheering minions after the news broke that Howard would be in the lineup. The team won all three games during his stay and since that time had scored at least five runs in more than half of their contests.

Hal Hansen, the team's director of promotions and the person responsible for my being in attendance on this particular Tuesday night, greets me and my family at the team's main office. He hands a pair of tickets to my wife and son, who will watch the game from the stands rather than try to shadow me as I venture all over the stadium this night. Hansen then ushers us way down the first-base line and into the passageway that leads to the "back of house" area, which contains a few batting cages and a supply closet that doubles as the interns' break room. Within that room is a door to the smaller area wherein resides the team mascot, Buster—or rather Busters.

Yes, this is where we see the fur-covered shell of Buster hanging from a chain hung high in the ceiling above, alongside two other backup Busters—older incarnations of the character's costume that the team uses for outside appearances. That fact is immediately gleaned by reading the warning sign posted at the rear wall of Buster's chamber, which clearly states, "Please DO NOT Take Any Part of the Newer Buster Suit for Appearances. If You Aren't Sure Which Is the Newer Suit, ASK SOMEONE."

Of course, I immediately wonder who that SOMEONE might be, as the suit that Hal points to as being the "newer" one is hanging next to a sign that reads "OLD BUSTER." However, far more confusing to me are the twin realizations that Buster is neither a crab nor blue in any discernible way. Instead, I quickly ascertain, he is bright yellow and clawless.

So what exactly is Buster? Apparently, I am told, he *is* a crab. A furry crab with fingers. I decide that, as a guest, I won't argue.

My family heads to their seats behind home plate as I continue on with Hal to take part in the pregame meeting, where all of the game-day staff learn what promotions are taking place and where and when they need to be situated to ensure everything goes off without a hitch.

Hal lets everybody know that the gates are going to open at 6:00 and then the Lillian Dean Dance Studio will perform on the field starting at 6:25. He also reminds the scoreboard operator that at some point—any point—before they start, they need to play a video provided by the Village Lutheran Church, whose parishioners will be singing "God Bless America" during the seventh-inning stretch. Apparently, the group's previous attempt to get their moment in the sun had been delayed by an act of God, namely that old baseball bugaboo, rain.

They are being squeezed into tonight's program, which is a very special night in Lakewood. Yes, tonight is the Bobblection. In a portmanteau of a promotion taking place at ten different minor league parks across the country, the first one thousand fans who enter the stadium will be given their choice of either a bobblehead of Barack Obama or one of Mitt Romney. The team has been supplied with five hundred of each, and the first candidate to run out will be declared the winner.

Apparently, a Bobblection has been held twice before, and both times it has correctly determined the eventual winner of the actual presidential election. We'll find out the results at the end of the second inning, but whichever bobblehead wins, I feel fortunate that neither candidate is actually in attendance that night. The last thing I need is to endure a repeat of the "kill shot" fiasco from 1997's Jackie Robinson Night at Shea.

The last item on the agenda is, well, me. Hal introduces me to the crew, many of whom probably haven't been paying close enough attention to notice that I am there in the first place. He briefly details my mascot bonafides and lets everyone know I'll be doing the regular Buster duties that day, which will start with his entrance at 6:35, riding in the backseat of a Mini Cooper. He then runs quickly through a list of other items, such as who's sponsoring certain giveaways and whatnot, then mentions something about a puppet show, whose performers' late arrival is made known to him by a blaring walkie-talkie. Hal needs to go off to find them, and just like that the meeting is adjourned. He quickly introduces me to a young kid who looks an awful lot like Clark Duke from *The Office* and *Hot Tub Time Machine* and leaves me in his hands. "This is our Buster," Hal says. "He'll show you where you need to go."

Matt Macnab was hoping to enjoy his final summer prior to his senior year at Toms River North High School. He had applied for, and gotten, an internship with the BlueClaws with the idea that he'd be learning how to use video equipment. Unfortunately for Matt, the guy who had been Buster for the previous few seasons quit just before opening night. Apparently, he left a message on Hal's answering machine telling him he got a job managing a restaurant and would not be back. The lack of two weeks' notice left the team in a bind.

For the first game, a different intern had been assigned to put on the suit and be Buster. He left at the end of the game and never returned. So when Matt arrived to work the next day, the team told him to take off his polo shirt and khakis and threw him some clothes from the gift shop. The rest, as they say, is history.

Although being a mascot was nowhere near Matt's cup of tea, he also was not a quitter. So he dug in his heels and did the job to the best of his abilities, despite not having any experience to fall back on. He ended up enjoying the work more than he thought he would, but certainly doesn't mind for a second that I'll be wearing the costume on this night instead of him.

*   *   *

WE GO DOWN TO THE CHAMBER OF HORRORS and Matt helps me get into the body of the costume. With so many snaps and buttons and clasps, it would have taken me until well after the final pitch to figure out the proper fastening sequence, so I am glad for the assistance. Matt offers up a choice of three different sets of hands, each pair rattier than the next, so I opt for the one with a small hole between the index and middle fingers on the left hand, simply because it has the fewest missing snaps.

Our suiting-up process is briefly interrupted by some yelling in the storage room. Apparently, a member of the clubhouse staff had claimed two bobbleheads for his very own and stashed them in his duffel bag, which he hid in this room for safekeeping. With most promotions, nobody cares if employees take home a few of the giveaway items, but voter fraud is not something to be taken lightly! His scolding over, the culprit sheepishly retrieves his bobblehead bounty from his bag and returns the dolls to the gates to be counted properly.

Crisis averted and democracy saved, it's time to complete my transformation. With body and hands in place, Matt helps me with the head, the sight of which, for some reason, reminds me in this moment of a drunk Fozzie Bear. I am now Buster. But before heading out into the world, I decide I need a moment to take stock of how I feel in my new skin.

Quite honestly, I'm not happy. The head just doesn't sit on my head quite right and tends to tip a bit forward. The body needs to be taken in about an inch on the shoulders in order for gravity to not have its way with it. Either that or I need to gain 40 pounds pronto, and since I've only recently begun to flirt with 130 on the scales, that's highly unlikely.

But I'm only renting for the night, not buying the Buster suit, so it will have to do. I give Matt the thumbs-up and we slowly make our way through a door on the other wall of the "supply closet" and enter the BlueClaws' clubhouse.

Baseball players are a notoriously superstitious bunch and this team is no exception. As we make our way through the room and head toward the door that leads to the area behind the outfield wall, reaction is immediate. Whether they actually notice Matt strolling alongside me and know someone else is in the costume or it's just obvious that somebody two inches shorter is in the suit, the verbal abuse comes ever the same.

"Honey, who shrunk the mascot?"

"You lost a few inches, Buster . . . and you're not as tall either."

"Look at that ugly thing . . . and Buster, too."

Several players come up to me to perform their various ritualistic interactions. Not knowing exactly what each player is expecting, I simply follow their leads and respond with as much gusto as I can. A fist bump here, a back slap there, two "secret handshakes," and a few fake bat swings at my head later, we are out of harm's way and off to my chariot.

There's no elegant way for a mascot to ride in the back of a convertible Mini Cooper. Seat belts are out of the question, and you kind of just have to grab on tight to whatever you can and hope the wind created by the speed of the vehicle doesn't either rip your head off or suck you out the back of the car.

Of course, you still have to wave to the adoring fans calling your name as you go, even if you are completely unable to turn your head to see them. Remember, I'm looking through a thin strip of mesh hidden amidst the fur of the costume's neck, with no peripheral vision whatsoever. I'm just taking it on faith that I'm not waving to empty seats and that the voices I'm hearing aren't in my head, the result of oxygen deprivation or heat stroke. Since I've only been in the suit for about ten minutes now, that seems unlikely.

The grounds crew has apparently forgotten to move a hose completely off to the side of the field and I'm nearly catapulted into low Earth orbit when the car slams on the brakes without warning. Luckily, my death grip on the backseat remains true and I avoid turning Buster into Travis Pastrana. However, my left shoulder certainly doesn't appreciate how close it comes to being ripped from its socket.

Slowly, the car resumes its trip toward home plate, so I can only assume the roadblock has been dealt with. Matt, who is sitting in the passenger seat, turns to me and says, "We're here!" Taking that as my cue, I attempt to extricate myself from my ride as graciously as possible, but still being unfamiliar with how large a radius Buster's personal space actually takes up, I catch my shoes twice on the front seat before stumbling forward onto solid ground again. It's far from triumphant, and my face grows red inside the costume when Matt has to come around and refasten the jersey to my furry frame.

Free at last to roam around and perform, the next few minutes are the high point of my evening. I get to interact with people in the crowd, sign autographs for the gaggle of kids who line the fence at the side of the field, all screaming my name with an urgency that only youth can muster. I go out to the right-field foul line, where the BlueClaws are doing their pregame calisthenics, and join in with the routine.

The players are more than amused by this and make room for me in the line, shouting words of encouragement and tipping me off to what is coming next, partially to help the show and partially, I imagine, so that I don't turn the wrong way and accidentally cause a chain reaction of catastrophe.

Hal is on the field with a microphone and he calls me over to take some photos with the multiple sponsors' representatives who are each going to throw out an "unofficial" ceremonial first pitch. My shoulder is really starting to stiffen up and I'm hoping that things can move along a little more briskly as I start to lose count of how many people come to the mound to take their turn.

Suddenly, Hal directs everyone's attention to the outfield wall, where someone, or rather something, has arrived to deliver the base-ball for the "official" ceremonial first pitch of the game. It turns out I am not the only dinosaur scheduled to appear on the field tonight, as the "puppet show" hinted at earlier turns out to be a life-size ani-matronic *T. rex,* who snorts and roars his way toward the pitcher's mound while the entire crowd reacts with amazement.

Accompanied by a woman straight out of *Crocodile Dundee* speaking in a farcical Aussie accent and dressed in her outback sur-vival gear, the beast takes his place about twenty feet in front of home plate. The handler carefully places the ball in the *T. rex*'s mouth and the beast "throws" it toward Matt Campbell, a pitcher with a 5.60 ERA who appears to have drawn the short straw that night.

Campbell seems a bit rattled by the whole affair, and I have to admit, even though I know the *T. rex* is just a guy in a suit—heck, *I* am just a guy in a suit—its realism makes me hesitant to approach the beast. Later in the game, Campbell will pitch an inning in relief, giving up a run on three hits. It will be his last action of the season, as two days later the team will give him his unconditional release.

The prehistoric display finally over, the umpires come out on the field. I make my way to the Lakewood dugout, exchanging fist bumps with the players as they take the field for the start of the game. Then, it's back to home plate, where, with my hand across my heart, I stand alongside the men in blue for the traditional singing of the national anthem.

Finally, at 7:05, when the home-plate umpire cries out "Play!" I exit the field through the home dugout and make my way slowly back into the bowels of the stadium below. Once back inside the supply closet that Buster calls home, I remove my hands and head and see the world through my own eyes again for the first time in what seems like an eternity. In actuality, it has only been forty minutes from start to finish.

I feel old, and it doesn't get any better sitting in a room surrounded by a gaggle of interns who are too engrossed in their own affairs to even acknowledge my presence. They're busy discussing all of the important issues of the day: who has been seen talking to whom and what she's going to say when she finds out he said that about her. It's typical teenage gossip, only without a clever Kristen Bell voiceover to help keep me engaged as I wait for Matt to return with a hot dog and a pretzel for me to devour before heading back out again.

Matt comes back as the talk turns to the cinema, specifically, "O-M-G! Did anybody ever hear of this movie from, like, thirty years ago called *Red Dawn* with that old guy from *Ghost*? It was so good!" I actually saw that movie in theaters when it was originally released in 1984. I was younger then than these kids are now. I offer up that they are shooting a new version of the film that is going to be coming out around Thanksgiving, and the kids are shocked to learn not only that I know what film they are talking about, and that I have heard of Chris Hemsworth and Josh Hutcherson, two of the stars of the upcoming remake, but mostly that I am willing to talk to them at all.

Apparently, as they are now quick to open up to me and share, it hasn't been more than a week or two since they were visited by Ted Giannoulas himself, as the Chicken made his annual appearance at the stadium. They were more than happy to divulge that he had been less than friendly. As one intern sums it up, "Two words. Di. Va."

When I later ask Hal about the Chicken's appearance, he has nothing but good things to say about him. "He is a highlight of the season for us," Hal says. "The fans love him and he puts on a great show. We always look forward to having him back." And of that, I have no doubt. Nobody questions that the Chicken is great at what he does on the field. That's never changed. But I guess his personality out of the suit hasn't changed much over the years either. I ask Matt if Ted gave him any advice, and the only thing he could remember him saying was "Stay out of my way."

At this point, it's time for me to resume my Buster duties. My new young friends and I are joined by a man in an audaciously ugly floral-print suit. This, I quickly learn, is Finkel. Finkel has been working at the stadium "since day one"—which, for this team, means 2001—and he handles all of the in-game emcee duties for the Blue-Claws. At one time, he was the announcer for the Harlem Globetrotters and performed in front of sellout crowds all over the world. He'll be more than able to keep the energy of tonight's crowd of 7,407 from petering out.

I follow along with Finkel, racing onto the field as soon as the last out is made in the top of the third inning. Armed with some T-shirts, which I toss into the seats toward the outstretched hands of eager fans hoping for a free souvenir, we quickly dart across the edge of the diamond, from the home dugout over to the visitor's dugout, within which we will make our hasty retreat.

Dugouts are always a tricky enterprise for a mascot. After all, with impaired vision, should you miss that first step, no amount of padding can brace you for the fall that will follow. And in all my days as Mr. Met, I was rarely met with anything but apathy when I did my little dance and flirted with that doomsday drop. Much to my surprise, and pleasantly so, as I get near the dugout of the visiting Delmarva Shorebirds, I hear several players call out: "Steps! Three of them!" And they verbally assist me down each one. "Step. Step. Step. You're good! Nice job."

We go back into the tunnel behind the dugout, where we hold firm, waiting for the middle of the fifth inning, at which time we need to go back out on the field for the singing of "Happy Birthday" to all of the kids in attendance who have paid for the privilege of an on-field Finkel serenade and a picture with the beloved Lakewood mascot.

Somewhere in that limbo, word comes back to us that Mitt Romney has been declared the winner of the evening's Bobblection, with a 4 percent margin of victory. In fact, Romney has carried the day in six of the ten ballparks in which the event is being held. Once the actual votes are counted in November, it will mark a clear and decisive end to the string of predictive successes this particular endeavor has enjoyed.

Eventually, the sound of approaching children pulls me from my self-imposed mini-hibernation, and before too long we are out on the field again: me, Finkel, the birthday kids, and for some reason that is never explained to me, three people dressed in hot dog costumes.

We go back down into the dugout, again with an assist from the Shorebirds. It's now time for Matt and I to venture out on our own, as we have reached the point in the game when Buster takes the elevator up to the stadium's SkyBox level to visit each and every one of the luxury suites and meet and greet the fans and corporate sponsors who are watching the game from far above the rest of the crowd.

Matt doesn't know the exact number of boxes there are and my memory on the subject is a bit fuzzy, but I'd estimate there are somewhere between twenty and twenty thousand. I mean, it just never seems to end. Door after door after door. Matt knocks loudly on the entrance to each suite, then throws it open, taking a huge step back in the process so I can make a grand entrance, to the shock and/or delight of the residents within.

Reactions run the gamut. There are children who run up to give me great big hugs, typically with hands covered in pizza sauce, cotton candy, or some other sure-to-stain substance. Other kids shriek in terror and only peek out sporadically from behind the safety of a parent's pants leg.

I take particular delight in the twenty-year-old who is equally terrified by my presence. She freaks out at the merest glance in her direction, yet cannot help herself from staying in the interior portion of the room that does not look out over the field. If it is truly that scarring an experience, she can easily go back out through the glass doors to the adjoining stadium seats where she was blissfully existing before my arrival.

Then there's a suite full of corporate muckety-mucks. Most of them leap up immediately to take their photo with me, but one guy stands far away against a back wall and will not approach unless I answer one question for him first. "Are you a guy or a girl? Guy or girl? Which one are you?" he asks. Naturally, I don't talk, so I simply nod and point at myself.

His fellow muckety-mucks are begging him to simply join the group photo, but he refuses to do so, and I refuse to clarify the answer for him, perfectly content to continue pointing at myself as if to say, "I'm Buster. I'm me."

"No, no. That's a guy in there," he says. "No, it's a girl. Which is it?!? Guy or girl? Why won't you tell me?" He doesn't appear to be drunk, only agitated. The bizarre behavior continues until I make my escape, a serenade of apologies from his friends following along after me.

Eventually we make it down to the final two suites, at which point I begin to relax. The ordeal—at this point, I am definitely no longer enjoying myself—is nearly over. I should know better than to let my guard down, but as out of practice as I am, that's exactly what I do.

Just before we knock, the door to one of the remaining unvisited suites opens from the inside. Upon seeing me standing there, a squeal of delight emerges from a woman cradling a sleeping newborn in her arms. Before I can even react, she has already handed the child off to me and is reaching into her pocket for a digital camera to commemorate the occasion.

This, of course, terrifies me.

There are two main reasons why I make it a personal rule never to hold babies for photo ops. First, there's the risk of what parents assure you is your No. 1 fan actually going No. 1 all over your costume, leaving a permanent stain and stink behind. Beyond that, though, is the fact that in the mascot costume, with oversize hands and a less-than-perfect grip, the ease with which I might accidentally drop a child is quite astounding. That's especially true when you add in the likelihood that an overexuberant fan, unaware of the fact I am carrying precious cargo, might well choose that exact moment for a sneak attack from behind.

Thankfully, both Buster's suit and the child survive the impromptu photo session, despite problems with the flash that necessitate multiple retakes. But if I wasn't physically drained enough before, I'm certainly down for the count after the stress of that situation. I make quick work of the final suite and then make my way as quickly as possible back to Buster's lair to extract myself from the suit once and for all.

It's somewhere around the eighth inning at this point, and I've been in the suit for about ninety minutes, give or take a few, on this hot August night. The BlueClaws are trailing 4-2, and I have nothing at all left in the tank to try and rally them. Sitting there, half in and half out of the costume and drenched in sweat, listening to the interns continue to discuss who is going out with whom and what they heard about what so-and-so put as their Facebook status and what it meant, just one thought echoes in my head.

I'm too old for this shit.

CHAPTER NINE

In Which We Learn That Baseball Is Indeed a Business

WHEN JOHN ROUTH WAS IN JUNIOR HIGH SCHOOL, he was like most teenage boys—completely unable to think clearly in the presence of a cute girl. So when Mary Foster, the prettiest member of the cheerleading team, asked him if he wanted to be the mascot for the Hand Hornets, how could he possibly refuse? Besides, his own brother had crafted the costume's head the year before. Little did he know at the time how that schoolboy crush would permanently alter the course of his life.

When Routh was a student at the University of South Carolina, one of the fraternities created a mascot named Big Spur to ride on its homecoming float, and after that parade, Big Spur started attending the school's football games. But the athletic department was concerned about liability issues arising from having an unauthorized mascot at athletic events, and in 1980 they decided to phase in Cocky, a cute but dumpy-looking barnyard chicken of their own creation. Routh was given the "honor."

The reception given to this unsolicited change in mascots was poor to say the least, so much so that the school decided to allow Big Spur to continue to perform at football games while relegating Cocky to "minor sports" like women's basketball and men's baseball. It was during a performance on the diamond that Routh's work caught the eye of the NCAA. He was invited to travel with the team to Omaha for the College World Series.

"While I was there, I got to meet coach Ron Fraser of the Miami

Hurricanes," Routh said, "and he was really impressed with the way the crowd responded to my performance. After seeing what I could do, he decided he was going to create his own mascot character called the Miami Maniac, and the next April he came to watch me work as Cocky in South Carolina. I guess they were having a problem finding a decent performer. You can't just put a guy in a suit and expect positive results."

Fraser invited Routh down to be the Maniac for a weekend series against the Florida State Seminoles. To say it went well is an understatement. "The crowd was expecting the Maniac to just stand around, because that's all he'd done," Routh explained. "I got out there and . . . did stuff. There was an audible gasp from the crowd."

The following year, South Carolina again made the trip to Omaha, but was eliminated from the tournament early. The Miami coaches asked Routh to stay on as the "unofficial mascot of the College World Series." Routh recalls that they took off the jersey identifying him as being from South Carolina and stitched together two T-shirts from the souvenir stand. Miami won the trophy and Routh celebrated with the team.

Fraser invited Routh, who was graduating, to come to Miami to work full-time as the Maniac. But South Carolina didn't want to lose Routh either, and offered him a free ride to attend graduate school if he'd remain with the Gamecocks. Routh was torn, so he sought counsel from one of the few people at the time who knew what being a professional mascot was like. Routh paid a visit to the Chicken.

Routh's cousin knew the general manager of the Spartanburg Phillies, then Philadelphia's Class A affiliate in South Carolina, and invited him up on the same night that Ted Giannoulas was going to be doing his celebrated shtick at the stadium. "I got there early. When Ted arrived, here he was in the middle of the summer in the hottest city in the world, and he's wearing a brown sweater vest. I was hot just looking at him," Routh said. "I stood up and told him that I was a mascot too, and he got an expression on his face that just screamed disgust and he muttered, 'Oh, no. Not another one' under his breath. Then when the GM came in and formally introduced me it was suddenly a different story. He was friendly and scheduled a time to talk to me after the seventh inning."

When Routh knocked on the door at the prearranged time, Giannoulas's handler answered and reluctantly allowed him to enter. "There he was, sitting alone in the dark, still in costume except for the head, which was perched on a table next to him. I asked him for some advice about the big decision I had to make and he leans forward and says, 'Yeah, I got some advice for you. If you ever do one of my routines, you'll never work in this job again. You heard me! Don't copy my stuff or I'll sue your ass.' I just politely turned and left. What a jerk!"

In the fall of 1982, Routh decided to go to Miami, and he remained with the university until 1993, performing not only as the Maniac but also as Sebastian the Ibis at football games during the Jimmy Johnson era. Routh says that one of the highlights for him came in 1985, when the baseball team was on a twenty-four-game winning streak, one short of the school record, and ESPN decided to air the team's attempt at making history.

The team had previously scheduled a mascot event for that game, which went on as planned—a wedding between the Maniac and the soon-to-be Mrs. Maniac, which looked suspiciously like the backup Maniac costume, only with lipstick and a wig. When the game was temporarily delayed for the nuptials, ESPN decided to stay with the action instead of going to commercial. "They ended up airing the entire thirteen-minute ceremony," Routh says with pride. "It was hilarious. Sebastian was the best man, and we had other local mascots like Grimace and the Hamburglar from the nearby McDonald's in the wedding party."

When the Florida Marlins joined major league baseball as an expansion team in 1993, they wanted to grow on the baseball experience fans in the Miami area were used to, and thanks to Routh's decade of work for the Hurricanes, that necessitated the creation of a mascot. Thus, Billy the Marlin was born—and there was no other choice for who would get to bring this fish to life.

"We had so much fun with Wayne Huizenga as owner," Routh said. "He was so easygoing and believed in the concept of having fun and making sure the crowd was entertained. I even got him to come out on the field and do the Hokey-Pokey with me. He got it."

As Billy the Marlin, Routh got in trouble only once, when a comedy bit he had done successfully in the past fell victim to unfortunate bad timing. "I had done this routine before, where I get up on this ladder and stand above this fake city, kind of like an homage to *King Kong*," Routh said. "Well, this one time, we tweaked it a bit because there was this big Godzilla movie coming out. So I jump off the ladder and stomp over the city and spray Silly String like I'm breathing fire. Unfortunately, the starting pitcher for that night's game was Hideo Nomo, and he happened to walk by at exactly that moment. We got some angry letters from some Asian American groups thinking we were making fun of him, but really, he had nothing to do with it."

Luckily, at the time, Routh was working for a team whose management "got it" and didn't make a big deal about it. That would soon change. Huizenga sold the team to John Henry in 1998. Henry wanted very badly for the Marlins to build a baseball-only stadium rather than continue to share a venue with the NFL's Dolphins and play in a building that really wasn't appropriate for baseball.

In order to do that, Henry knew he'd need some help in terms of funding and support from local government. That meant a lot of schmoozing, and having a masterful public relations tool like Billy the Marlin could go a long way toward getting the job done. He gave Routh a three-year contract to continue working his mascot magic. But in January of 2002, Henry took advantage of a chance to buy the Boston Red Sox and sold the Marlins to Jeffrey Loria, who was happy to sell his Montreal Expos team to Major League Baseball, as at the time it appeared that the Canadian team was due to be "contracted."

With Loria came David Samson, his stepson, who was named team president. Samson wanted to meet all the current staff in order to see if they wanted to retain anybody's services, since they were planning to bring most of the staff from Montreal with them to Miami.

Routh's first impression of Samson left more than a bad taste in his mouth. "He calls me in and, even though he's eight years younger than me, demands I call him Mr. Samson. I mean, Wayne let me call him Wayne. But, okay," Routh says. "So he asks me what I do. I tell him I'm the mascot. He says, 'No really. What do you do?' Did he really not know what a mascot was? I joked that I basically dress up and act like an idiot. 'No, seriously, what are your duties?' [Samson asked him]. Clearly, he just didn't like me."

Although he was allowed to work the 2002 season, Routh knew he probably wasn't standing on the firmest ground when it came time to negotiate a new contract. "One of the VPs called me into his office in October and told me they were not renewing my contract, that they were 'going in a different direction,'" Routh said. "I asked him who made that call and he said it was David Samson. I said I wanted to talk to him, which I think took them by surprise."

Routh went to Samson's office but was told he wasn't there. "I took a few hours to clean out my office, pack up my car, and calm down a bit," he said. "When I went back to see Samson, he seemed really scared, like I was going to beat him up or something. I said, 'David, this is what's called groveling for your job.' No reaction. I offered a 50 percent cut in pay. I really just wanted a year to get myself situated and plan for the future.

"Plus I really thought there was a good chance this team was going to win the World Series in 2003. The last thing I said before I left was 'I want to be standing on the field with you, David, when we win it all next year, and give you a great big hug.' He said he'd think about it and give me a call in a few weeks."

The next day, Routh's phone rang at 7:00 a.m. He let it go to voicemail. It was Samson telling him there was nothing left to work out and requesting that he leave his badge at the gate as soon as possible. And so it came to pass that for the first time in almost twenty-five years, John Routh would no longer be wearing a costume. Ironically, his last day on the Marlins payroll was Halloween.

* * *

FEW MASCOTS GET THE CHANCE to bow out on their own terms. More often than not, the hatchet comes down unexpectedly, either via an early-morning phone call or, in my own case, via e-mail.

When I first started as Mr. Met, I was paid about $30 per game and the going rate had not increased all that much during my first three seasons on the job. I believed what I was doing was worth so much more, however, and I wanted to really transform the mascot job into something that could eventually become something a lot more permanent for me.

Before the start of the 1997 season, based on research I'd done on how other teams were running their mascot programs, I presented the team with a proposal for creating a mascot coordinator position, with the idea that I'd be the one to fill it. It looked something like this:

MASCOT COORDINATOR: A full-time position

SALARY: $32,500 and full benefits

HOURS/VACATION: This is not a nine-to-five, forty-hour-a-week job. This job will sometimes require working as many as twenty-one consecutive days, extensive travel, and frequent performances at night and on weekends. Due to the unusual nature of the position, liberal time off is to be given.

JOB DUTIES

1. To perform as mascot at all home games, or to see that a proper replacement is obtained in the event of an emergency

2. To coordinate between all relevant departments throughout the course of the season (including, but not limited to, promotions, community relations, video/scoreboard, marketing, and stadium operations)

3. To actively pursue appearances and publicity for the mascot at outside venues, and to appear at said venues, or to see that a proper replacement is obtained in the event of an emergency

4. To schedule said appearances, plus any arranged by other departments and to prioritize any conflicts that might arise

5. To represent the New York Mets in a positive manner with the public and/or the press at all times

To their credit, the team took my proposal seriously. A few months later, they offered me significantly less money than I had requested and no benefits, and they gave me a new boss—Kerry Kaster. They had basically hired Kerry to handle all of the duties I had outlined, save the actual getting into the suit and performing.

I was given an "office"—essentially a workstation on the press level in a room shared by the entire scoreboard staff, Kerry, and me—and was told that I was "on probation." After the season, the team would revisit the necessity of my position being worth more than fifteen bucks an hour. I was told that there was a budget for props for the season and asked to come up with a list of skit ideas for approval. Also, I was to make as many cold calls as I could in order to turn Mr. Met into a moneymaking enterprise—in essence, to pay for my own salary—by booking as many appearances as I could.

Here was the main problem. Any skit I came up with that required a prop had to be signed off on by Kerry, since he controlled the prop budget, and all routines had to get the okay from Tim Gunkel before we attempted them on the field.

But there was no give-and-take.

As a jumping-off point for brainstorming, I'd offer up an idea like getting a fishing pole and dangling a giant dollar sign in front of the Marlins' dugout when they came to town, in order to poke fun at the fact that former Mets star Bobby Bonilla had just signed a huge contract with them via free agency. But instead of this triggering an exchange of ideas, I would simply get told by Gunkel, "No, I don't like that one."

When the Boston Red Sox came to town for their first-ever interleague series with the Mets, I suggested we have a guy in stilts come out to the field in a Boston uniform and walk to first base. Then, I'd have asked Mookie Wilson, our first-base coach at the time, to walk with me to home plate and "hit me" with a bat, sending me trickling down the first-base line, where I would run through the stilt-man's legs and into the outfield—a larger-than-life recreation of one of the most iconic moments in team history, namely Game 6 of the 1986 World Series.

That one just drew blank stares, and I was told that it didn't matter because it had already been decided what my hilarious skit would be. All during the game, for reasons I can't recall, Diamond Vision was planning to showcase a video retrospective of the 1996 season over the course of several inning breaks, culminating with footage of the World Series, which had been won by the hated Yankees. So, just before the image of Charlie Hayes catching the final out of the decisive Game 6 was shown, the video screen would go black. That's when I was to emerge from behind the centerfield wall carrying a ginormous plug in my hand, laughing hysterically at the "prank" I'd pulled.

Not only did I not think that was in the least bit funny, I also questioned the whole presentation of the bit. Nobody would really think the power had gone out, because all the other lights in the stadium, including the ones above the video screen, were still going to remain on. Plus, I pointed out, how would anyone know to be looking at the centerfield wall when I appeared? Most people, I argued, would miss the whole thing.

"Well, we'll put a camera on you and show you on Diamond Vision so they won't miss it," Gunkel said.

"You mean the same Diamond Vision that I supposedly just pulled out the plug on and am still holding in my hands?"

"It doesn't matter. We've already paid $500 for the plug to be made and so we're doing it," Kerry blurted out, ending the discussion.

This was the way the whole season went. When I brought a broom out on the field to celebrate a sweep, as I'd done every single time the Mets were lucky enough to win all three or four games of a series against a visiting club over the past few seasons, I was told via a voicemail from team VP Dave Howard, "That's not what this organization is about" and instructed not to do it again. What aren't the Mets about? Winning? Celebrating a win? It made no sense to me.

About halfway through the season, Gunkel told me he was a bit concerned that I wasn't doing enough outside appearances. I asked him what I was supposed to do about that. All of the appearance requests that came in were directed to Kerry, and whenever I asked for an official quote on how much I was supposed to charge for any appearances in the event that I did manage to book one, I was told that it was to be determined on a case-by-case basis and that I'd need to let Kerry "take care of things" from that point. In other words, I was told I was not allowed to book appearances in the middle of being reprimanded for having not booked any appearances.

The low point of the year for me was when my roommate, John, who worked at the Mayor's Office of Film, Theatre, and Broadcasting and was in charge of approving all film permits around the New York City area, told me a writer from *Mad About You*, a popular sitcom at the time, had been talking to him about a story idea they'd recently had for the show. In the script, Paul Reiser's and Helen Hunt's characters are finding it impossible to get their baby to sleep, so they end up driving the child all over the city in the middle of the night. The writer thought it would be funny if the exhausted parents happened to drive past Shea Stadium, see Mr. Met wandering around in the dark, have him pick up the crying infant, and have it immediately fall asleep.

John told the writer that he knew Mr. Met personally and helped initiate contact with me. What a coup! Mr. Met, who was still an unknown quantity in most of the country, was about to get national television exposure. Of course, I didn't have final say in the matter. It had to go through Kerry, who said he didn't feel comfortable approving it without sending it up the chain of command. By the time the request made its way back down the flagpole, the Mets—in their infinite wisdom—had decided to ask the show to pay a couple thousand dollars for the right to use Mr. Met for the cameo. I was stunned, but the show was more than stunned. They were insulted, and they wrote the mascot gag out of the episode entirely.

And don't get me started on the fact that Mr. Met didn't have a dedicated mode of transportation to get me to the rare appearance that did manage to cut its way through all the red tape and actually come to pass. If we wanted to go off-site, we needed to borrow the old blue van that Pete Flynn and the grounds crew used to transport sod, soil, and fertilizer. The vehicle had only a driver's seat and one front passenger seat—everything else had been stripped clean so as to maximize the amount of cargo space.

With Kerry claiming driving duties and a cameraman sitting shotgun with his equipment in his lap, I was left to hang on for dear life in the back of the death trap, being thrown from side to side as we barreled down the highway and doing my best not to have any part of my costume actually make contact with the filthy residue left behind after the van's most recent trip to the local garden center.

The most extreme example of Gunkel and I butting heads took place in August of 1997. He wanted Mr. Met to ride on a float in the Dominican Day Parade in Washington Heights, a neighborhood in northern Manhattan. In theory, I was not opposed to the idea, even though most people in that area tend to be Yankees fans. The primary problem I had with the plan was that the parade would take place at the same time as a home game.

Not being able to be in two places at once, I argued that it was far more important to be at Shea. Gunkel didn't agree. Of course, he probably never saw a mother and her eight-year-old daughter sprinting down several stadium ramps, screaming for me to stop just so the young girl could get a hug. I'm not saying I was the reason most people came to the park, but quite frankly, for fans of a certain age, I very well might have been. To not even make an appearance on the field and ruin the day for even one family was not worth it, as far as I was concerned.

But again, my opinion carried little weight, and so Mr. Met piled into his, ahem, limousine, being driven by some underling from the promotions department. With a game going on at Shea, everybody else—from Kerry Kaster to the cameramen and even my intern bodyguards—was deemed to have more important things to do back at the stadium. At least I finally got to ride shotgun.

When we arrived, I discovered that the float they wanted me to ride on was not being sponsored exclusively by the Mets, as I had been told, but rather was cosponsored by Presidente Beer, an iconic brand from the Dominican Republic. I had my chauffeur get on the phone with his supervisor in a last-ditch effort to call the whole appearance off, but she didn't understand why I had a problem.

Call me crazy, but I didn't think it was such a good idea to have the Mets mascot—to whom children are naturally drawn—riding on a float endorsing alcoholic beverages. Since I couldn't convince anyone to cancel the gig, I refused to board the float and instead opted to march behind it, to lessen the connection between me and Presidente.

For a whole city block, things were actually going great. The merengue band on the float played a catchy little tune that the lead singer punctuated every so often with a shout of "Go, Presidente!" and it was fun to dance along, waving to the crowd. However, I was unaware that this was no ordinary merengue band. I don't recall what their name was, but apparently, in the Dominican community, they were bigger than the Beatles. As soon as we crossed the first intersection, the throngs of parade-goers standing on the sidewalks toppled the police barricades and, as one, started streaming toward the float to get as close as possible to their beloved Juan, Pablo, Jorge, and Ringo.

Suddenly I was swept up in the onrushing crowd and pinned to the back of the float. Luckily, my costume, especially my oversize noggin, afforded me some protection. For the rest of the seemingly never-ending parade, I did a survival samba, trying to avoid being trampled while simultaneously dodging the onslaught of would-be drummers who mistook my head for a giant conga. The humiliating experience only worsened when the singer for some reason changed his chant from "Go, Presidente!" to "Go, Yankees!" about halfway through the route. Somehow, I escaped serious injury and we eventually made it back to Shea Stadium—several hours after the game had ended.

I later learned that over the following few weeks, the team received several phone calls and letters from upset parents whose children were heartbroken that Mr. Met had not been at that day's game. But I'm sure the team simply explained to them how their kid's weeping jag was worth it because it's far more important that Mr. Met help a beer company endear itself to Yankees fans than to make sure people leave Shea with a positive feeling and want to return time and time again.

All is forgiven, right?

* * *

A FEW DAYS AFTER THE END OF THAT 1997 SEASON, I met with Tim Gunkel in an otherwise vacant Shea Stadium. In spite of everything, I was still hoping to continue on as Mr. Met for at least one more season, but the wear and tear on my knee was worrisome. All I asked for was to be given health insurance, and if that happened, I'd be happy to make the Mets my No. 1 priority year-round. If not, I informed Gunkel, I'd have to take on some other freelance work in order to be able to pay for it myself, and therefore might not be available at the drop of a hat when—if—those outside appearances happened to magically manifest themselves. Gunkel told me that I was considered a seasonal employee and as such, not eligible for benefits. I asked him if he could ask someone higher up the food chain if an exception could be made in this case, and we agreed to meet again as the season approached.

On January 5, 1998, I received this e-mail from Kerry Kaster:

> Hi AJ. Before someone else informs you, I wanted to be the first to let you know that we have conducted a job search for a full-time Mr. Met, and that we have decided to offer the position to a candidate from Cincinnati. His name is Derek Dye, and he has some good experience in the performing arts (including performances at Kings Island), as well as some much needed experience in handling the administrative end of the job. I look forward to working with Derek in making Mr. Met more visible and a true marketing tool of the company. As you know, it will certainly be a challenge.

I couldn't believe what I was reading. Although I was perfectly prepared for the eventuality that I had already served my last moments in the Mr. Met costume, I certainly did not fathom the idea that I would be fired in this cold a fashion. It was going to take a few days to sink in before I could formulate a coherent response to Kerry.

Imagine my surprise and confusion when just two days later I received an e-mail from Vito Vitiello outlining specific times and dates for my upcoming appearances for the Mets Caravan, a promotion in which, on the first day of ticket sales, a handful of Mets players traveled to various locations around New York City in order to create buzz for the upcoming season before they made their way down to Florida for spring training. This year's itinerary even included a visit to *The Rosie O'Donnell Show*.

Vito asked me to get back to him as soon as possible to inform him of any conflicts. Now this was interesting. Apparently, not only had Kerry wanted to be the first to let me know I had been fired, I was also, apparently, the only person he had informed of this fact. Needless to say, I was more than a tad bit ticked off. After taking a day to sleep on it, I was no less angry about how things had gone down.

I decided that I would, in fact, discuss things further with Kerry and sent him a reply indicating my disappointment that after four years with the organization, not a single person had felt it necessary to offer me the simple courtesy of telling me that a search was being made to find a new Mr. Met. In retrospect, I guess I should have expected as much from the Mets because, on the whole, most of the people in charge thought that all I did was put on a costume.

Kerry eventually sent me an apology for not picking up the phone and actually, you know, telling me I was being fired at the time the decision was made. However, he also told me that both he and Tim Gunkel had questioned my commitment to the job and my ability to see the big picture. "The position shouldn't be about AJ Mass and his comfort level," he wrote. "The position should be about developing and publicizing Mr. Met."

Looking back on my firing, even with the advantage of hindsight, I still feel like I was far more in the right than not. The Mets were upset that I was unwilling to commit all of my time to the organization, to essentially be on call 24-7-365 to jump into the Mr. Met costume whenever they needed me to. Yet, when I asked for health

insurance to be added to my compensation package, I was specifically told that I was not eligible for coverage because I was not a full-
time employee.

I therefore needed to schedule other work in order to supplement my income so I could afford to pay for the benefits they
refused to provide me with because I was not a full-time employee,
and they took offense at that because they felt my decision to do so
meant I was shirking my responsibilities as a full-time employee.
That's not a lack of perspective. That's an inability to exist within
such a paradox.

To that end, I would agree that it was financially irresponsible to
continue to pay me what they were, given the existence of Kerry's
job. But it was equally unfair of them to judge me for not performing
these duties when they had explicitly handed them to somebody else.
But that's par for the course in Major League Baseball.

* * *

ED MCBRIDE FOUND HIMSELF FACING A SIMILAR CONUNDRUM at the tail end of his
run as Dinger, the dinosaur mascot who helps root on the Colorado
Rockies at Denver's Coors Field.

McBride actually got his start as a mascot in college, at East Carolina University, after his attempt to walk on to the baseball team
failed. "I didn't make it and I had a lot of free time on my hands," he
said. "A friend of mine told me about the mascot auditions and
thought I would be great at it, so I gave it a shot." Ten to fifteen people showed up to the initial audition, and each candidate was asked
why they wanted to be the mascot. "Everybody said they had never
done this before and I simply said that I was really looking forward
to being the mascot, and I think my confidence really spooked a lot

of them," he said. "Most of them didn't come back for the second day of the tryout, so I got the job sort of by default."

After three years as the ECU Pirate, McBride attended a mascot camp run by Dean Schoenewald. If that name sounds familiar, it's because Schoenewald was the mouthy twenty-five-year-old who ran for mayor of Ocean City in 1985. Schoenewald had always wanted a career in sports, and when he saw the Chicken and the Phanatic make it big, he just knew he was meant to be a professional mascot himself. The day before he was set to go off to North Dakota State University, where his intention was to walk on to the hockey team, Schoenewald instead phoned his regrets to the school and used his tuition money to construct his own costume.

It was a sight to behold. Coming in at about seven feet tall, adorned with white feathers and a beak, and with a "#1" emblazoned across his chest, Schoenewald marched right into the headquarters of the Philadelphia Eagles and offered up the services of the character he called Bird Brain. The Eagles declined, though they did say they couldn't stop him from buying a ticket and showing up to games in the costume—so that's what he did.

Schoenewald never missed a game, and would sometimes even be seen wandering around outside the stadium when no game was being played. On one occasion, he was set on fire by a Dallas Cowboys fan during a *Monday Night Football* game, but he remained resolute in his attempt to convince the team to hire him as their official mascot. He kept up the act through his failed effort to become mayor and a short stint as a local TV weatherman. But after ten years of constant pushback from the Eagles, he'd finally had enough.

In 1991, hearing that there was a new NHL expansion team in the works—the San Jose Sharks—Schoenewald once again took his life savings out of the bank. He spent close to $25,000 constructing a shark costume and drove across the country to try and convince the team that he was the right man for a job that didn't even exist yet. The Sharks were not entirely convinced, but nevertheless they allowed Schoenewald to perform in his costume—and he took things to an extreme level, bungee jumping from the rafters of the team's home arena at the time, the Cow Palace (though it turns out that death-defying stunt was actually performed by somebody else due to Schoenewald's fear of heights).

Overall, the antics made quite an impression, but in an interview Schoenewald gave to a Philadelphia weekly newspaper in 2001, he said that when the team asked him to improve his skating skills he told them to "kiss my royal ass" and left.

From there, Schoenewald became a bizarre nomad, if his outlandish stories are to be believed. He was hired by the Ottawa Senators to be their mascot in their debut season of 1992, but did not have the proper work visas required for an American to be employed in Canada. So, he claims to have snuck across the border by paddling a boat with a hockey stick so he would not miss his debut. During his short time in Ottawa, Schoenewald's performances received more pans than raves, and his contract was declared null and void. He sued the team for "$125,000 in lost wages, $25,000 for mental distress, $100,000 for damage to his reputation and $5,000 for the Stanley Cup ring he might have been able to win," according to *Philadelphia City Paper*.

In 1993, he turned up in New Jersey as mascot for the Devils. This time the reason he gave for deciding to walk away from what he alleged was a six-figure contract was because the team had asked him to shoot T-shirts into the crowd and he felt it was "beneath him." That's not the story that has become part of NHL mascot lore, however. One former hockey mascot told me that Schoenewald is used as a cautionary tale, and that the incident that actually prompted his dismissal was when, in a game against the then-Disney-owned

Anaheim Mighty Ducks, he fired off some sort of blank gun into the rafters and had dummies of Mickey Mouse and Donald Duck plummet to the ice below, dead on arrival.

As the article went on to recount, after controversy followed him during minor league baseball gigs in both Vermont and Nashville, Schoenewald decided to open up his own mascot camp in 1996. McBride found out firsthand that people weren't exactly knocking down the door to get trained by him.

"It was really just a weekend in Nashville, just me and him—not even a group," McBride recalled. "Getting one-on-one training did seem a bit odd, but he had heard through the grapevine that the job in Colorado was opening up and told me about it, though he added that he didn't think it was a good fit for me. I think he was just a bit jaded and told me that the business was hard and that you should make lots of demands and get paid a lot for doing what mascots do. I just wanted to have fun, and I think that was why he didn't really encourage me to go for it."

The Rockies weren't exactly all that enthusiastic about McBride going for it either. After receiving McBride's audition tape, they called him back and said they were really interested in getting somebody who was local and already a fan of the team. McBride was stunned. "I told them they should be looking for a good performer who wants to be in the costume. Baseball is the hardest sport, with eighty-one dates and very long games. You don't need a fan. You need someone with talent."

Two days later, they called McBride back and told him that his words had really resonated with the selection committee. Although they'd already completed their local auditions and had a winner in mind, they said they'd hold off making an official decision if he could fly himself out that weekend to put the suit on and do some crowd work at an event the team had scheduled.

Due to the short notice, McBride ended up having to buy himself a $1,000 ticket from North Carolina to Colorado, but it proved to be money well spent. Calling it the easiest audition ever, McBride won them over and for the next five-plus years called Coors Field his home.

"It was so much fun, those five and a half years. I would not trade it for anything," McBride reflects. "But little by little, they began to take that fun away." Part of the fun when McBride began his tenure was his interplay with the Rockies' manager at the time, Don Baylor. Though he had a very gruff exterior, Baylor actually possessed a terrific sense of humor. When McBride first suited up as Dinger, Baylor harassed him endlessly whenever he performed in front of the Rockies' dugout, hurling expletives his way and taunting him with an incessant "You're not funny. That's not funny. Boo!"

I had experienced the acid barbs of Baylor myself, having heard the screams of "You can't dance! You call that dancing? You suck!" coming from the Rockies' dugout on the few occasions the Rockies visited Shea while I was Mr. Met, so I knew firsthand what McBride was talking about. One day, McBride was sitting in his dressing area before a game, reading a mystery novel and trying to relax a bit before suiting up. "Baylor walked by and then doubled back and just stared at me until I looked up," he said. "Then he said four words before walking away: 'The wife did it.' I was so pissed. When I went on the field, I brought the book with me, and then tore it into pieces and threw it at Baylor. 'Okay, now, that's funny,' he said. We were finally cool after that."

They were cool, at least, until Baylor got the axe after the 1998 season. Baseball is, after all, a transitory game for all those who wear the uniform, save the mascot. As for McBride, his responsibilities grew over time to where he was in control of the majority of decisions relating to the character's schedule, except for management's insistence that Dinger visit each and every luxury suite during each and every game. McBride arranged a meeting with a team VP to discuss returning a bit more flexibility to his game-day duties.

"I understand you need to make the sponsors happy, but for me, the job is all about interacting with the fans," he told the VP. "I can't do that spending five innings up in the suites every game. And it's not like those people up there are any less important, but in many cases it is the same people in the same suites every game. It makes it tough to do the character. They're always there. They're not going to get upset if I don't stop by all the time."

When McBride was told that was simply how it was going to be both now and in the future, he decided that he needed more money to do the job if they were going to take away a huge chunk of both his autonomy and his enjoyment. The team said that in that case, they'd be happy to look for somebody else. In the course of an hour, McBride's time as Dinger came to an abrupt end. The meeting started at 4:00, that day's game was to start at 5:00, and McBride walked out the door at 4:45.

Today, McBride programs point-of-sale computers for a living. Although he does miss being in the spotlight from time to time, there are some things he's happy to have left behind. "I can't stand sweating anymore," he said. "I don't ever want to be covered in sweat again. But I miss the relationships and seeing those fans who would always give me that certain unique high five.

"There was this one time, a girl who was in a wheelchair gave me a huge hug," McBride said. "At the time I only remembered her because her dad was kind of distinct, but about two months later I see the dad on the concourse, and I'm ready to walk down to their seats to see his daughter again, and he just grabs me and starts bawling. He told me his daughter had died earlier in the week, but that she talked about the time Dinger played with her at the stadium all the way up to the end. It was one of her happiest moments. The team has no idea what we do, how much impact we have. *That's* what made leaving so hard."

*   *   *

LEAVING THE MARLINS WAS HARD ON JOHN ROUTH as well, and it only got worse when the team did in fact go on to win the World Series in 2003. "I didn't watch a single minute of it," Routh said. "I just couldn't. You become this character—I mean, you know you're a person inside a costume—but it becomes your identity. And when it is suddenly ripped away . . . how can you not have some bitterness?"

He considered filing a lawsuit against the Marlins due to the fact that several other employees who were let go as a result of the change in ownership were given severance packages based on the length of their tenure with the club, but in the end, he decided it wasn't worth the effort.

Time heals all wounds, though, and his firing gave Routh an opportunity to go back to the University of Miami, where he currently works as the executive director of the school's Sports Hall of Fame. "Coming 'home' really helped me to move on," Routh reports. "I can go out there and see Sebastian and the Maniac performing cheers I created. That's something special that nobody is ever going to be able to take away."

CHAPTER TEN

The Elephant and the Glass Ceiling

PERHAPS IT'S NOT ALL THAT ODD that the vast majority of professional mascots have been men. After all, why should this job be any different from the rest of the real world, where opportunities for female advancement in certain industries are typically hampered by some sort of glass ceiling. Let's be honest. If women had trouble being accepted in the worlds of doctors and lawyers, nobody should be surprised to learn that an occupation that depends on a high level of personal interaction with male athletes might also be slow to warm to them.

Sure, there are some very real physical demands that come with the job of mascot, and perhaps a higher percentage of eligible candidates might end up coming from the pool of those with a Y chromosome for that reason. However, making that genetic profile a prerequisite for getting the job is an idea whose time should have long since faded away, no? I mean, one would hope that by now we've moved very far away from the sort of paternalistic thinking that prevents women from doing jobs they are every bit as qualified for as men are.

In 1990, however, society was light-years away from where it is today in terms of its sensitivity to issues of gender equality. *Pretty Woman*, a film that reinforces the myth that all a "hooker with a heart of gold" needs to have a happy life is to find a wealthy man to take care of her, was tops at the box office that year, and there were only two women serving in the United States Senate (as opposed to

20 today). It was against that cultural backdrop that Rana Lee Araneta began her freshman year at Syracuse University.

Araneta had arrived in central New York by way of Hicksville, Long Island, where she had been the "president of everything" in high school. Her first foray into extracurricular activities in college led her to the marching band, but after watching Otto the Orange in action, she had an epiphany. "He looked like he was having so much fun," she said. "He was so free! He was running around and the whole stadium was his and he could go wherever he wanted and I was, like— that was it. I just decided in that moment. I wanted to be him. 'That's totally what I'm going to do next year.'"

Unfortunately, as she began to ask around about the audition process and how she could achieve her goal, Araneta learned that this was totally not going to happen. The mascot at Syracuse had always been under the purview of the Lambda Chi Alpha fraternity. In the 1950s, the father of one of the fraternity brothers made a costume for his son to wear at games, thus beginning a four-decade tradition of Lambda Chis serving as the mascot at all Syracuse sporting events.

But Araneta was not about to accept the news of the fraternity "owning the rights" to the mascot and simply find something else to do. "I was like, 'No. I've already decided I'm going to be the mascot,'" she said. "So I told them it was wrong. 'Times are changing. You can't just block a student who is totally psyched to be the Orange from even trying out.'"

The fraternity was caught between a rock and a hard place, not wanting to discard a tradition that was a huge part of the fabric of the fraternity's chapter, while at the same time not wanting to come across as sexist. Araneta says that Linda Bell, the cheerleading coach under whose auspices the mascot job fell, understood that she was not going to go away quietly. That's why, she believes, a deal was quickly struck between the fraternity and the university that opened up tryouts to the entire student body. Three students would be chosen in this fashion, with Lambda Chi Alpha retaining the right to select an additional two of their own brotherhood for the remaining members of the "team."

Just as she wanted, and even before auditions began, Araneta soon found herself at the center of attention on campus, but perhaps not in the way she had envisioned. The *New York Times* ran a story on her having been the impetus for the change in how the school handled mascot auditions, and soon thereafter she started to receive anonymous hate mail and death threats.

At the same time, however, she received a ton of support from the female population on campus, who were not only happy to help try to boost her morale and shield her from verbal abuse, but were also willing to assist in her actual audition. "At that time in my life I had so much energy. I had to perform an acrobatic routine, a skit, and a dance. My entire floor showed up and helped me to create an obstacle course and I ran around all these orange cones I had painted with swirls and stars," Araneta recalls fondly.

When all was said and done, Araneta became the first female mascot at Syracuse. While she was received warmly by the rest of the mascot team, including the Lambda Chis, she nevertheless soon found herself on the receiving end of glares and cold shoulders from the female cheerleaders. "Maybe they just hated me because they were all starving themselves to look 'perfect' while I got to pig out," she offers up, only semi-seriously.

* * *

OF COURSE, NOT EVERY CHEERLEADER is of the mind-set that the position of mascot is beneath them. Jaime Stoeckle's cheerleading career at

Santa Teresa High School in San Jose, California, was built on a mascot foundation. "When the time came for cheerleader tryouts, I didn't have a partner," she said. "So there was this other girl there and she was trying out for the mascot and asked me to team up with her. So we made a costume, got together a routine, and tried out."

Stoeckle didn't make the team as a freshman in 1991, but was successful the following year, proudly prancing around that season dressed up as a St. Bernard. She attended spirit camp in the summer and got specialized training as a mascot, but then went back to her original plan and spent the next two years as a cheerleader. Still, her mascot past ended up paying dividends.

"I went back to spirit camp after my senior year and took the mascot workshop as a cross-over elective," she said. "The instructor remembered me and invited me to come back the following year as a mascot instructor." Some cheerleaders may have taken offense, but not Jaime. She embraced the opportunity, and doing so paid off for her in a huge way.

After her second year in the program, the president of the company called her up with a proposition. He had learned that the Oakland A's were looking for a new mascot performer and he suggested that Jaime throw her hat in the ring. "I never thought I would perform as a mascot professionally," she said. "I actually kind of had an 'in' with the San Francisco 49ers to be a cheerleader and was going to do that. But he really wanted me to try out, so I felt I should go."

Jaime and her mom drove up to Oakland from San Jose and met with the A's director of marketing. After a brief tryout, he offered her the job on the spot. "I was stunned," she said. "I had just kind of gone there to see what would happen, and he was like, 'We want *you*,' so that's where I ended up." And that's how a girl who went to A's games with her father as a child became the first female major league mascot at the tender age of nineteen.

The A's flew Jaime out to New York to get fitted for her costume—made by 3/Design, which also made Mr. Met ("We shop at the same store!" Jaime joked)—and on April 4, 1997, Stomper the Elephant, a kinder, gentler, cuter version of Trunk, made his debut. What Stoeckle best remembers from that night, though, are the tears.

Stomper's introduction to the fans came by way of having the character rappel from the outfield bleachers all the way down to home plate. They hired a stuntman for that particular task, so the first time anyone saw Stomper, it wasn't her. She had to stand there and watch as this uncoordinated guy attempted to dance, post-landing, and made a horrible first impression.

Once it was finally her turn to get in the suit, nothing seemed to go right. The tights that came with the suit didn't fit properly and some of the snaps didn't quite reach where they were supposed to connect. The costume's head didn't have a helmet or anything, so it simply bounced around all over the place, and the eyes, through which Jaime was supposed to be able to see where she was going, fogged up instantly, leaving her blind.

"I was so young and I didn't know anything and I was so overwhelmed and that day people were pushing and shoving and grabbing and they're so excited and I wasn't 'one with the costume' yet and I had no idea what I was doing," Jaime said. "I was in there—and I was just crying inside the suit." Stoeckle can laugh at the memory now, but at the time, she remembers thinking she was prepared to quit on the spot. *Get this over with,* she thought. *This is the worst thing ever. I hate this. I don't want to do this.*

While eventually Jaime got the hang of being Stomper, it was definitely overwhelming for her at first, especially because the Oakland organization felt the need to saddle her with so many rules. "People think it is so easy: Just put on a costume and run around," she said. "But don't go over to the players and don't do this and don't do that. Now, go out there in the middle of the field and entertain."

The other edict from management that Stoeckle had to deal with wasn't necessarily unique to Oakland. The A's wanted her identity to remain a secret. Nobody was supposed to know who was inside Stomper's costume. However, they took this one step further. They didn't want anybody who worked for the team to know who she was either. "I literally knew only three or four people," she recalled. "I mean, I didn't expect to be paraded around the office, but it was like, I don't know, just a little odd. I'm this young kid, I have no idea what I am doing. I'm working for this professional team. Like, 'Oh, by the way, don't tell anybody what you do. Pretend you're an intern.' What is that?"

It wasn't until after Jaime met the rest of the "gang" at the 1997 All-Star Game that she realized it wasn't the end of the world if she told some people that she was the mascot. Before then, she was totally isolated at the stadium, with her changing room in the back of a storage closet and absolutely no contact with the players, as she was kept far from the locker room due to her gender. But, filled with a new confidence after being accepted by her comrades in costume, Stoeckle mustered up the courage to approach Mark McGwire at the luggage carousel when her plane landed back in Oakland.

"I kind of walked slowly up to him and introduced myself as Stomper," she said. "It was so cool because he was so nice to me. He started asking me all these questions. How I got the job, what it was like. I think he must have went and told everybody on the team about it, because the next home stand, I went down on the field and Jason Giambi came up to me while I was in costume and said, 'So I heard you're a girl.' And slowly, the players would give me high fives and Miguel Tejada would play catch with me and I think they started to realize I wasn't going to embarrass them. I was just there to do my job."

I asked Jaime what it felt like, being the first, and at the time only, female in the entire group of major league mascots. "I was so young," she said. "I was still such a little girl. I was told I could bring a guest with me to Cleveland for the All-Star Game and I brought my mom. But everybody seemed cool and I felt that I played the little sister role, so people were very protective of me—in costume and out."

To that point I can personally attest. I remember an incident in Kansas City when a group of mascots who had gathered for Sluggerrr's (the Royal's mascot) birthday party were walking through the stands, and Stomper got caught in a group of abusive fans. With some of the veteran guys, we probably would have just let them handle it. But we knew that Jaime was in the suit, so we instinctively all doubled back and helped extricate her from the situation.

"Overall, being a girl, I didn't feel it was a disadvantage in terms of the mascot community, because everybody was so supportive," she said. "So, I mean, they were all just open arms: 'Let's help you, let's teach you, let's take care of you.' I mean, I'm sure some of them were trying to get in my pants, but I mean, whatever."

In some cases, Jaime is quick to add, being a girl is an advantage. Although mascots don't usually talk in the costume, when a fan got a little too aggressive or would shove or kick her, Jaime wasn't above firing off an occasional "Hey, listen, buddy. I'm just a girl in here." That usually resulted in red-faced remorse. *"Oh, god!* I'm *so* sorry!" But that was only a last resort for her. Normally, when asked directly if Stomper was a boy or a girl, Jaime would pantomime something that tipped the inquisitor to the fact that Stomper was a boy, because *he* was, even if Jaime most definitely was not.

After four years on the job, all that commuting back and forth between San Jose and Oakland for games and outside appearances while also working her way through a full course load at college began to take its toll on Jaime. However, an offer of full-time employment from the team certainly gave her reason to reconsider. And when the A's invited her to the company picnic, it appeared that she was finally being accepted by the organization. That is, until the other shoe dropped and Jaime learned that the invitation was to come to the ferryboat soiree in costume as Stomper—she was the only employee being asked to work the party rather than to enjoy the experience.

In 2000, when the San Jose Sharks offered her an event coordination position—one that didn't require her to wear a costume and had a much shorter commute—the time was right for Stoeckle and Stomper to part ways. But that didn't come without one more secrecy-related snafu.

Oakland made the playoffs that year for the first time in eight seasons. When she arrived at the stadium to suit up as Stomper, she was turned away at the door. Apparently—and I wouldn't know myself, having not worked for the Mets during a season where they played on into October—employees of playoff teams get a whole new set of credentials before the postseason starts. Jaime, who did not work out of the stadium office, had not received her new documentation. So, even though she was holding the Stomper costume in her hands, and even though the same security guard had let her in many times before, she was forced to sit there and wait until somebody with the proper clearance could come down and officially identify her. And it was no easy task, given the stealth mode that permeated all those years she spent pretending to be an intern.

✷ ✷ ✷

WHEN IT COMES TO KEEPING A LOW PROFILE, Kelly Frank is simply never going to get on board. She's just too outspoken a personality, for better or for worse, to do so. Frank originally became a mascot at her high school because it looked like it might be fun, and before she knew it, she was getting paid to entertain crowds at professional sporting events all over South Florida.

Unfortunately, Frank seemed to be a bit cursed, as the teams she worked for had a strange way of disappearing shortly after she began cheering them on. The Florida Bobcats of the Arena Football League folded in 2001, the Miami Fusion of Major League Soccer was contracted that same year, and the Orlando Miracle of the WNBA relocated to Connecticut following the 2002 campaign.

Undaunted, Frank continued to pursue the business of being a professional mascot. After a season of working for the Brockton Rox in the unaffiliated minors, she was hired to work as the backup performer for the Tampa Bay Rays, ultimately earning the full-time job in 2005. Frank was great inside the costume, but it was her realization that using social media and the Internet could really build a following for a team's mascot that led to huge growth in the popularity of the Raymond (not to be confused with *Dave* Raymond) character she embodied.

However, just a month after the Rays played in the 2008 World Series against the Philadelphia Phillies and hearing from team management that Raymond had outperformed the Phanatic in their eyes, Frank was unexpectedly dismissed from her position. "I had been offered positions for more money in previous years, but turned them down out of loyalty to the Rays. It wasn't about the money for me," she said.

Apparently, though, for the Rays it *was* about the money. They had allegedly fired the original Raymond, Shawn Christopherson, in 2004 because of his high salary. Now, it seemed they were cutting costs again. "It depends on the team and the individual executives, but if somebody new comes in that has a different perspective, you're screwed," Frank said. "Unfortunately, that mentality of 'put an intern in the suit' is pretty prevalent."

The Rays' run to the playoffs came in the first season following a change in ownership that saw Stuart Sternberg take over the reins from Vince Naimoli, the man who had been awarded the expansion franchise in 1995. Frank was apparently a casualty of that regime change, an all too familiar tale in the mascot world. As Glenn Street once said, "The downside of the mascot is that you're probably the easiest person to replace because you can slip somebody inside the costume and nobody may know the difference."

In fact, Frank says she did her job so well that few people outside the organization were aware of the gender of the person inside the Raymond costume. "Most people assumed it was a guy, although there were some times when my gestures would give me away. But I always tried to play it up where I would flirt with both men and women and keep it a mystery."

Frank was not out of work for long, and in fact, she didn't even have to leave Tampa to continue her career, as she was soon hired as ThunderBug, the mascot for the NHL's Lightning. Hockey proved to be a very different experience for Frank, who found the job to be a lot more challenging than performing during baseball games. "Hockey is fast and slow at the same time," Frank said. "There's no set time for you to go on. You perform between whistles. So you always have to wait, do your stuff quickly, and then sit down."

Frank's tenure as ThunderBug came to an abrupt end in January of 2012. During a game against the Boston Bruins, ThunderBug went up to a fan of the visiting team and sprayed him with Silly String. There's nothing inherently nefarious about such an assault—it doesn't permanently damage a person's clothing, nor is it really all that embarrassing in the grand scheme of things—but nevertheless, the "victim" did not find the incident the least bit amusing.

He burst out of his seat and, from behind, he shoved Frank, who had already turned to leave the area, into the railing on the stairs. Security came over to make sure the incident didn't escalate and escorted the Bruins supporter away from the scene and out of the arena.

It wasn't the incident itself that got Frank fired, but the fact that she tracked down the in-house video of the conflict and posted the footage on YouTube. Although she had not intended for the video to go viral, that's exactly what happened. Frank didn't really want to talk about it, but hinted that once again, with new management then in charge, the team was looking for an excuse to let her go and simply took advantage of the negative publicity generated by the video to justify ending her employment with the team.

This was not the first time a fan had been physical with Frank, and she had complained in the past that security tended to be a bit nonchalant about coming to her aid. But because she had indeed violated the organization's social media policy, she takes full blame for getting the axe. Besides, Frank was ready to move on. She felt there was a huge difference of opinion between her and the team about how best to promote the mascot and that she had no more room to grow if she stayed.

"It's very hard to do this as a career, and it's harder than when I started," Frank said. "Even somebody who thinks they're a super gymnast or a great dancer, their chances of getting a job are still pretty slim. Certainly you can if you really want to—go for it. But the lack of job security is very real. I've been making costumes forever, so at least I had that as a fallback."

Indeed, Frank now devotes her time to running her own company, Amazing!! Mascots, which designs and builds costumes for teams like the Houston Astros as well as minor league teams and local businesses across the country. She says that, for now at least, her days as a mascot performer are through.

* * *

LEAVING STOMPER BEHIND was a bit harder for Stoeckle, but not because she wasn't also ready to move on. Instead, she was concerned that some of the fans she left behind might not understand why things had changed. "Stomper had friends around the ballpark," she said. "We had secret handshakes. I knew where they sat. I would go see them every game and we'd do our little rituals. I didn't like the feeling that the next time they saw Stomper they wouldn't get that special attention I always gave them."

Jaime especially worried about one special kid named Brian. Every year, Stomper would visit a camp for kids who have muscular dystrophy. In costume, she had bonded with Brian, bound to his wheelchair and a staunch fan of the rival San Francisco Giants. Over the course of several summers, he warmed up to the cute little elephant to the point where he would not leave Stomper's side.

"'You're my best friend,' he'd say to me," Stoeckle tearfully remembers. "And knowing I would never see him again, or any of the people I had developed relationships with . . . not being able to thank them or say goodbye, *that* was the hardest part for me."

But being the center of attention? *That's* the part of the job that Stoeckle had no problem leaving behind. "What's great is that, especially now, a lot of people want to be famous," she said. "They think that fame and celebrity is the coolest thing ever. And it was really unique because as a mascot, I was the most famous person in the ballpark, so to speak, for those four years. If I went somewhere, people were screaming for my picture, wanted my autograph, wanted to come talk to me, wanted to come give me hugs."

"But twenty minutes later, out of costume, I could walk the same path of the stadium and nobody would say a word to me," she continued. "So I got the celebrity and I got the taste of it, which was fun, but in reality, do you really want somebody coming up for your autograph when you're trying to pump some gas? Not really. So, I've tasted it. I wouldn't want to taste it for the rest of my life, be Britney Spears, because she can't go anywhere. I got to feel the rush of it for a while, but then go back to reality once I got out of the suit."

Stoeckle worked for the Sharks for five years after leaving the A's. There, everybody on staff knew her name and what she did. However, she was laid off during the 2004 NHL lockout and eventually moved on to a career in real estate, which not only pays more, but also allows for a lot more flexibility in scheduling. That comes in handy, because Jaime Stoeckle is now Jaime Chapin, happily married and the proud mother of two boys.

Looking back, she has no regrets. "It was a cool job, but because I got in, got the magic, and then got out, I can be nostalgic about it," she says. "If you do it until you can't physically perform anymore, I think you probably become jaded. But when I think of Stomper, it just makes me smile. It was such an important part of my life and who I am and who I was."

But there was one incident from her time in the suit that, upon reflection, Jaime isn't too proud of. She had been dating this guy and got him a job as an intern for the team. Eventually, though, he also started dating her roommate, and a breakup followed soon after. However, for some reason, he decided to bring her "former best friend" to a game with him and put her on full display in the employee section.

Suffice it to say that Jaime was none too happy with this development. So, during the game, Stomper paid them a little visit, during which the mascot "accidentally" spilled a couple of large sodas all over the couple. "She jumped up and screamed that Stomper did that on purpose, which of course he did. But how is she going to prove it?" And since this was in the days before the ubiquity of the Internet, the incident did not make its way onto YouTube and Stoeckle lived to mascot another day.

✸ ✸ ✸

RANA LEE ARANETA NEVER really felt 100 percent comfortable as a mascot, in part because of the negativity she got from the cheerleaders who had resented her when she first started out. However, after three years as Otto, she felt a sense of pride in the fact that other girls started auditioning and getting selected for the role.

"It taught me about fearlessness and really inspired me for the rest of my life," Araneta said. "I did consider doing it professionally when I learned people actually did that for a living, but it got lost." After a short time living in Los Angeles, disillusionment set in for Araneta and she eventually bought a one-way ticket to Asia, where she simply traveled for three years in order to try and find herself again.

When she finally returned to the United States, she set up shop teaching yoga and meditation in Northern California. Before talking to me, she said she had pretty much kept her mascot memories stored away. "In the suit, it was Rana times a million. It's an amazing dichotomy. On the one hand, you wear this mask, but it actually magnifies *you* more," she said. "I think, for a while though, I was so focused on the negativity of those who didn't want me to succeed that I forgot about the joyfulness and the positivity of the experience.

"You just opened a whole box in my mind, man. I don't know if I would be who I am today if not for the experience of mingling with the spirit of Otto. It definitely propelled me to follow my path. I think revisiting those days after trying not to for so long has made me more free. I feel so much positivity psychically seeping into me now, and I can fully enjoy the truth about what I accomplished."

CHAPTER ELEVEN

Putting the "Con" in the "Confluence"

THERE'S A SAYING THAT GOES "It's easier to ask for forgiveness than it is to ask for permission." That could easily be the mascot credo. After all, we're always out there pushing the envelope and seeing how much we can get away with. It's in the very nature of what a mascot strives for, straddling that line between discord and rhyme, as it were.

Mascots live in a state of perpetual limbo. We're the face of the franchise, but never actually show our faces. We're the fans' representative on the field, but to the fans, we're part of the team—so we never truly belong to either world. Millionaires traveling on private jets aren't going to welcome us along for the ride, yet the fans see us as something "other" as well.

Then there's the lack of any true job security. If the act of performing a skit goes well fifty or a hundred times in a row, regardless of whether management had previous knowledge of the script, there's no problem to be found, and perhaps no acknowledgment that the performer has done anything special with their time on the field. Management might not even have been watching. However, get it wrong just once—and the complaints come rushing in and you may quickly find yourself yanked from the costume permanently.

How willing is a performer going to be to push the envelope and perhaps stumble across something special if they have no job security? Is a kid making ten bucks an hour going to care enough to put in the extra effort? The attitude of most sports teams who have thrown an intern into the fray is "He's just a kid. We can't give him any responsibilities." Except, of course, they have just placed this kid inside the biggest marketing tool at a team's disposal and sent him out there to interact with the public, where he has a real chance of alienating the customer base and perhaps psychologically scarring a kid for life because he really doesn't know what he's doing.

There's a huge difference in status between professional mascots who patrol major league sports arenas and the "Dirty Elmos" who skulk around the Times Square area of Manhattan in ratty, foul-smelling rental suits, offering to pose with tourists for a dollar or two. But that difference in status can only come over time, as public trust builds up through the long-term and consistently positive portrayals of these lovable characters by the men and women to whom the task of maintaining that community goodwill is given.

Yet because of the actions of a few bad eggs over the years, many organizations erect a cone of silence around the identity of their mascot performers. The New York Mets, for example, not only endeavor to keep the name of the current Mr. Met completely under wraps, but also take the veil of secrecy one step further.

Richard Sandomir, a reporter for the *New York Times*, told me that in the course of researching a story on the team's search for new investment partners to help offset the significant monetary hit the franchise took in the Bernie Madoff scandal, the Mets were surprisingly coy about the subject. The team was offering a bunch of perks to these potential investors, including "access to Mr. Met at Citi Field," presumably in the form of suite visits during games. However, not only would they not confirm the identity of the person inside the costume, they also refused to even admit that there was a person inside the costume at all.

Unfortunately, I can't completely blame the Mets, or any other team, for not wanting to have the identity of the mascot out there for all the world to see. As Kelly Frank learned the hard way, in today's world of social media a single act of mischief can spread like wildfire and result in unexpected and unwanted backlash.

It's not that hard to imagine a photograph of an out-of-suit mascot pounding back a few beers on his or her own time getting taken out of context and blown out of proportion when filtered through the lens of a rival team's fan hoping to cause some trouble. Of course, sometimes the "smoking gun" comes in the form of a snapshot taken while the performer is actually wearing the costume, as was the case when somebody tweeted a candid shot of the Kansas City Royals' mascot, Sluggerrr, getting a lap dance from a stripper. Although the out-of-bounds antics allegedly took place in 2005, the visual evidence didn't appear on Deadspin.com until March of 2013, and the current resident of the costume is going to be the one who has to deal with the public relations uproar.

It's true that not every mascot throughout history has been a model citizen outside of the costume, and it's not always something taken out of context that gets the performer in hot water and the media all worked up. Sometimes it's an actual felony.

● ● ●

THE RESURGENCE OF THE LONG-DORMANT Pittsburgh Pirates was one of the feel-good stories of the 2013 baseball season, marking, as it did, the club's first winning season since 1992, when they reached and lost the National League Championship Series for the third consecutive year. In the twenty-one seasons to date that have followed their dramatic Game 7 loss that year, the Pirates have employed seven different managers who, despite a few brief moments of optimism, have presided over no fewer than ten ninety-loss seasons, including, in one stretch, seven in a row.

While the beginning of the Pirates' woes on the field coincided with the departure of slugger Barry Bonds to the San Francisco Giants via free agency after the 1992 season, the greater truth is that a dark cloud has followed the team ever since they first made the decision to bring a mascot aboard.

After the huge success and buzz created by the Phillie Phanatic's debut, in 1979 the Pittsburgh organization invited Dave Raymond to the Steel City to help them introduce their own character, a Parrot, which seemed like the appropriate companion to hang out with a bunch of Pirates. Raymond does not recall the trip fondly. "I got to know the organization and, coming from Philadelphia, it was like walking into a prison camp," he said. "I mean, everyone was walking around so tense and it was just this immediate understanding that things were very different here."

Funnily enough, the first resident of the Parrot costume would one day barely avoid prison for real. Kevin Koch had always wanted to be a major league baseball player, but like many a youngster with visions of one day being enshrined in Cooperstown, that future simply never materialized. Still, he remained a big fan of the team, and when a friend told him that the Pirates were looking for a mascot, he decided to give it a shot.

The timing couldn't have been more perfect. Koch got to dance on the dugouts as Willie Stargell and the 1979 Pirates captured the imagination of the entire country. Using the song "We Are Family" by Sister Sledge as an anthem, they rallied from a three-games-to-one deficit to defeat the Baltimore Orioles and win the World Series in seven games.

They were the rulers of the baseball world as a whole, but in Pittsburgh, anybody associated with the team was treated as if they walked on water. That included Koch, who would later tell Bryant Gumbel in an HBO interview that he was part of that "family," hanging out with players in and out of costume and being able to have all the women and booze he wanted. Eventually, that decadence led to the 1980s drug of choice—cocaine. Many of the players on the team were users, and they turned to Koch to be a middleman of sorts, helping them to procure the drugs and deliver them to the clubhouse.

Eventually, the FBI got tipped off to the widespread use of recreational drugs throughout baseball and offered Koch immunity in exchange for wearing a wire during one of his "runs." He agreed, thinking he could save his job, but once the cat was out of the bag, the Pirates didn't want anything to do with him. Koch was fired and he fled the city.

But Koch was just the first in a line of Pittsburgh mascots behaving badly. In 1995, with almost a decade having elapsed since the infamous drug trials, Pittsburgh decided to tempt fate again, holding auditions for a second mascot to go along with the Parrot. This wasn't going to be a costumed character, but rather simply a "cheerleader" dressed as a swashbuckling buccaneer. Recent college graduate Tim Beggy beat out thirty or so other candidates to win the job.

Unfortunately, his reign was to be all too brief. In July of his debut season, Beggy was caught getting "a little too close" to a fan while swimming after hours in a public pool. The arrest, which was detailed in the local papers, ended up getting reported by ESPN and even found its way into Jay Leno's monologue on the *Tonight Show*. The team immediately relieved Beggy of his sword, and eventually he and his female companion both entered into plea agreements with the city and paid small fines.

Beggy ended up working part-time in the steel mills and bartending before another audition went his way. He was cast on the second season of MTV's *Road Rules*, a show where five castmates travel around in a Winnebago and are tasked with doing different physical challenges in order to win prizes. Along the way, word got out about Beggy's past and the quintet decided to break into a hotel swimming pool to reenact the inglorious event.

Obviously, the network didn't have as much of a problem with this as the Pirates had, and certainly had no qualms about airing it, either. But, due to the negative publicity that Beggy's original faux pas had caused at home, the Pirates never recast the Buccaneer and instead opted to let the character fade away into a hazy memory as quickly as possible.

During that time, the Pirate Parrot himself had actually managed to walk the straight and narrow. That all changed when Tom Mosser, who had been relatively—and mercifully—anonymous as the mascot in the post-Koch era, retired after the 1996 season. The Pirates' choice of a replacement, unfortunately, once again proved to be flawed, and it was not too long before the organization again found itself with a public relations headache on its hands.

Jeffrey Deceder was attending high school in Ambridge, Pennsylvania, a little more than fifteen miles outside of Pittsburgh, when his idea for the Parrot was hatched. He was fascinated by the costume and, since his school had no mascot of its own at the time, he decided to make one himself—emulating the Parrot costume but employing a red and gray color scheme instead of the green and gold of the Pirates' mascot. Deceder—Desi to his friends—enjoyed being the center of attention. He was a talented magician and juggler and a big fan of old-time comedy acts like Abbott and Costello. He loved entertaining people and relished being able to touch as many people as possible.

After attending Penn State University, a stay that did not include a stint as the scarf-wearing Nittany Lion mascot, Desi won a contest that gave him a chance to have his wedding at Walt Disney World in Orlando, Florida. He took them up on the offer and got married—with Mickey and Minnie at his side. He was so tickled by the whole experience that he decided to stay, taking a job at the theme park in which he dressed up as Pluto, Eeyore, and the Mad Hatter.

While in Orlando, Desi hooked up with Sports Magic, a company that dispatches performers to sports venues across the country, where they entertain crowds with T-shirt cannons and the like. Desi really took to the experience of barnstorming from stadium to stadium and interacting with fans on a personal level, and after meeting a whole bunch of professional mascots during his travels and finding them all to be friendly and willing to offer up encouragement about pursuing that line of work, he knew he wanted to become a full-time mascot.

He soon got his chance, as the Sacramento Kings were in the process of finding someone to fill their opening for a mascot performer, and in fact several of his friends in the NBA mascot community recommended him for the opportunity. He flew in for auditions, worked hard at learning how to do some of the aerial acrobatics required for dunking as well as taking a few dance lessons to improve his ability to cut a rug, and got the job. Desi's favorite part of each night, though, was the original skit he was allowed to perform.

"If the team had a seven-footer on the roster, I'd go out with stilts and tower over them," Desi recalled. "There was one night, I came out in a Rock 'Em Sock 'Em Robot–style contraption and got Charles Barkley to spar with me. Of course, I did some lame skits as well. For some reason, there were a bunch of sheep that would from time to time block the road outside the stadium, and so I did this 'Mary Had a Little Lamb' skit complete with a live sheep. That was horrible."

Desi also utilized his magic background by "transforming" a fan of the opposing team into a Kings fan with the wave of a wand. It was a fun environment full of challenges and the learning curve was steep, but Desi found being a mascot to be a perfect fit. "Most mascots are so willing to share ideas and help a newcomer to fit in. I was really enjoying myself immensely." However, when Desi learned that the Pirate Parrot job had opened up, the chance to return home and suit up as the mascot that first got him thinking about being a mascot in the first place, it was too much to resist.

And that's how Desi Deceder ended up succeeding Tom Mosser as the Pirate Parrot. The adjustment from basketball to baseball, though, was not without its speed bumps. "I had done basketball for so long and, you know, it's funny," he said. "When you're around hoops mascots, they think they're the best. When you're around baseball mascots—they think they're the best. Every community probably has that. But while basketball was all about the acrobatics and the flair, baseball really was more about the interaction with the fans. How can you not fall in love with hugging people for a living?"

Hugging can sometimes get you in trouble, though, and as much as Desi fell in love with the job, it didn't take long before the Pirates began to fall out of love with him. There was one incident in which a young child was pulling on the Parrot's beak, then moved on to his wing and then up to his hat. The kid just wouldn't let up, so Desi pulled the lad in close, put his beak over his head, and whispered, "Hey, please don't do that anymore." Of course, the sight of the Parrot "swallowing" a small child is an attention grabber, so all eyes were on the youngster when he decided to yell out, "The Parrot cursed at me!"

Incidents like that certainly don't win you any fans, even when you profess your innocence, and cumulatively they build up to the point that when a performer finally does something questionable that can't be denied, an organization will seize upon the chance to pounce. That's what happened to Desi. In his third season with the Pirates, he was making an appearance at a car dealership and decided it would be funny to take a convertible out for a test drive—in full costume.

"So, I'm riding around and honking my horn and waving to other motorists and people walking on the streets are getting a huge kick out of it when a cop sees me and pulls me over. In retrospect, it was not a good idea, but at the time, it felt like a great idea," Desi chuckles. The cop walked over, hand on his holster, and demanded that Desi "remove [his] head." Although it was embarrassing, the officer let him off with a warning. However, while Desi stood there headless at the side of the road, a Pirates fan who was a witness to the scene called a local radio station to tell the wacky afternoon deejays what was going on. Suddenly, the Parrot was "breaking news" and management had grounds for termination.

Desi and the Pirates soon parted ways and he returned to his basketball roots, performing all over the world as Globey, a mascot for the Harlem Globetrotters. The opportunity to experience all different cultures and societies was great, but Globey mostly did his stuff before the game started. Once the Globetrotters took the court, they didn't need a mascot to help keep the crowd laughing.

Apart from the occasional skit and pregame dance routine, Desi was nothing more than a glorified roadie, riding the bus with the Washington Generals—the team of players hired, in essence, to lose each and every game and be made to look foolish in the process. With Desi's second child having just been born, every time he made somebody else's kid laugh it only made him want to be back home more.

So the globetrotting was put on hold and for the next four years, Desi plied his mascot trade for yet another professional sport, entering the world of the NHL as Slapshot, the mascot for the Washington Capitals. Like several of the other mascot performers I interviewed for this book, Desi found hockey challenging. "You have less than thirty seconds to put on a skit, get your point across, and get out," he said. "In baseball, you have three outs to get to your next location. It could take a very long time. In hockey, the breaks are perfectly timed and you have to sprint to get to a different section of the arena before the next stoppage of play.

"Being a mascot is more of a lifestyle than a job," he continued. "You have games at night and appearances on the weekends. Family time was bringing my wife and kids with me when I performed. It's not easy." In 2006, that lifestyle came to a sudden end when Desi herniated a disc in his back and was no longer able to perform at the level required of a professional sports mascot. At least that's Desi's version of events.

There are two types of mascot performers—those who get inside the suit and become far more extroverted than they ever would be in real life, and those who don the costume and magnify those aspects of their own personality that were already there to an extreme level. I would consider myself to be one of the former group—if you were to meet me in person, you'd find me to be soft-spoken and very willing to let others grab the spotlight. Desi, as he himself would admit, clearly falls into the latter group.

Desi's tenure as the Pirate Parrot coincided with my time as Mr. Met. I know him personally and genuinely like him, but it was always apparent that he had an overwhelming need to be the focal point of any situation and completely in charge of everything. Any mascot gathering we were both at ended up with Desi being the one to plan the evening activities, and more often than not that meant a trip to a local strip club.

There's nothing wrong with that, necessarily. Strip clubs have never really been my thing, but as I was single and in my twenties at the time, it's not like I'd rather have gone to the library. But with Desi being in his early thirties and introducing us all to his nineteen-year-old girlfriend, let's just say he sometimes came across as a little creepy.

On April 26, 2007, Desi appeared on an episode of Dr. Phil McGraw's television show along with Jennifer—the girlfriend in question—who by this time had been married to him for more than a decade. The episode was entitled "Obsessive Love," and it painted a picture of Desi that was truly shocking.

Over the course of the two-part episode, it was revealed that Desi was so possessive of his wife that he tapped her phone and secretly placed a GPS tracking device in her car. Cameras and recording devices were found all over the family home. Jennifer said that Desi made it impossible for her to hold a job by turning off her alarm clock so she'd always be late and by calling her co-workers at all hours of the night and threatening them if they talked to her.

By the time Dr. Phil got Desi to admit he used a knife to make an incision in his body in order to fake a vasectomy so he could get her pregnant and force her to stay with him, it was clear that something was seriously wrong with Desi's mental health. Desi told Dr. Phil that Jennifer was also at fault, though, saying that "the attention that I need has made me into a person who grovels to her and begs for the simplest kiss. If she was more loving toward me and would show me some affection, I wouldn't want to do my behaviors."

Dr. Phil got Desi to agree to get professional help, but the damage to his marriage was already irreversible. Jennifer decided to get a divorce, and planned to inform Desi of her decision when the couple returned to the show one month later for an "update." However, Desi's doctors felt that he was in no condition to receive that kind of news, so a decision was made to keep him from seeing Jennifer during the taping of the episode. Desi did not react well to not being able to see Jennifer, and on his way back to the treatment center, while his car was stopped at a light, he threw open the door and ran off in an attempt to make it to the airport, in order to catch a flight and beat his wife home.

At the end of this nationally televised drama, Desi ended up in jail for two months for violating a restraining order. After the episodes aired, everybody in the mascot community was talking about them. Nobody could believe how far off the deep end Desi had fallen.

For the next few years, Desi kind of dropped off the grid, save a Facebook post he made in 2010 in which he talked about going on a thousand-mile-long unicycle trip to Iowa—where Jennifer had moved after the couple's divorce was finalized—in order to drum up support for his quest to regain custody of their children. At the time, Desi claimed he had not seen his kids in almost four years and was hoping his mission would aid his ongoing legal battle. As he wrote, "I want nothing more out of [this mission] than to know that thousands of people know my heart and will cheer so loud when I arrive in Iowa for court that everyone there will then see how loud my heart is crying for the chance to be the father my children love."

I honestly didn't know what to expect when I finally tracked Desi down and was able to talk to him in March of 2013. I asked him if he wanted to talk about the *Dr. Phil* appearance, and at first he declined. But he eventually reconsidered, sounding far more sad and defeated than sinister. "It was a decision I made to go on the show and put stuff out there," he said. "It definitely had a negative effect on my life. I wouldn't do it again. But at the time, I thought it was a good choice."

Desi felt the show was unfairly edited and focused far too much on making him the bad guy. "We weren't allowed to talk about certain subjects and it didn't air until five months after the taping," he explained. "It's a program for women and they could have made it a lot more evenhanded, but they didn't." I'm sure Desi isn't entirely wrong here—all television shows use editing to tell the story they want to tell, and perhaps all the warts they chose to include were Desi's—but when Desi lists his appearance on the program under his "acting credits" on the professional résumé he has posted on his business's Web site, you get a sense of the disconnect with reality here.

He told me he's currently living back at his childhood home, caring for his elderly mother and hoping that the hard times are now behind him. Over the years, Desi, for all his faults, did put a smile on a lot of people's faces. So for his sake, I hope he can indeed put the past behind him and move on.

● ● ●

BRENT GEPHART DID HIS BEST to rehabilitate the image of the Parrot and make it something to be proud of, rather than something to run from. "It's a tough transition to change the persona and not have the Parrot be thought of as the guy who was in trouble," Gephart said. "You have to work really hard to change that perception, and while it can take all of your career to gain some notability, it can take only one second to lose it."

Gephart had dreams of being an Olympic gymnast, having taken to the sport as a toddler, but a torn rotator cuff suffered while attempting an iron cross on the rings ended thoughts of gold at the age of fifteen. Even though his competing days were over, Gephart decided to stay involved in the sport as a coach in his hometown of Buffalo.

One of his students had an aunt who worked for the Triple-A Buffalo Bisons, and she thought that with his athletic background, Gephart would be a perfect candidate to be the team's mascot. He decided to give it a shot, and when he heard the crowd's reaction to the backflip he performed in costume, he was hooked. Gephart remained with the team for six seasons, until the director of promotions for the Pittsburgh Pirates, who had once worked for the Bisons, called him up in 2001 to see if he wanted to take over the role of the Pirate Parrot.

Gephart agreed and helped the team inaugurate the brand-new PNC Park. With a new stadium and a new performer in the costume, the Parrot got a makeover of sorts as well, becoming even more kid friendly than before. Although the first year was challenging for Gephart, team management under owner Kevin McClatchy—who had bought the team in 1996—gave him plenty of space to find his footing. The mascot flourished and began branching out with a road show that traveled all over the country and internationally as well.

"It was a family place. I wasn't from Pittsburgh, but felt very welcomed by everyone with the organization," Gephart said warmly. Eventually, however, the grueling work takes its toll on any mascot, and Gephart knew he wasn't going to be able to do those backflips into his forties. Before the start of the 2007 season, he sat down with McClatchy after months of agonizing internal debate and told him he needed to pass the torch to somebody else. McClatchy understood and even allowed Gephart to come back and perform at one final spring training game so he could get some sense of closure. Without any public fanfare announcing his departure, he simply stood in the outfield and soaked it all in. Then he did one final backflip and called it a career. Today, he remains in the greater Pittsburgh area in his new career as a realtor, having vanquished the Pirates curse once and for all.

Or has he?

You see, 2007 also marked the final season that McClatchy would own the Pirates. By the time opening day arrived, he had already sold a controlling interest in the team to a new ownership group led by newspaper magnate Robert Nutting. The first of Desi's *Dr. Phil* episodes aired just two weeks later. McClatchy announced he would step down as CEO in July.

* * *

IN JUNE OF 2010, a Pirates fan named Andrew Kurtz posted some comments on his Facebook page criticizing the ball club for having extended the contracts of the team's general manager and manager despite the fact that the team was mired in a twelve-game losing streak and already more than ten games out of first place in the National League's Central Division. Normally, that wouldn't be such a big deal. Fans always have bad things to say about losing teams. That's unavoidable. The problem was that Kurtz wasn't just a fan. He was also one of the team's mascots. Since 1999, in-game entertainment in Pittsburgh has included a pierogi race, in which four runners dressed in dumpling costumes race around the warning track to the cheers of the crowd, which is encouraged to predict the winner and vocally support their selection. For his efforts, Kurtz got $25 per race and a chance to see his Pirates play for free.

Four hours after his Facebook post, Kurtz got a call from the mascot coordinator of the Pittsburgh Pirates, informing him that he had been relieved of his pierogi-ing duties and requesting that he turn in his black Spandex pants at his earliest convenience. Kurtz apologized for his actions, but the decision was final.

Kurtz's mother thought the team was overreacting, though, and alerted the media to what had happened to her son. The media were quick to share that story with the entire city. Once again, the Pirates became the butt of jokes around the sports world thanks to the actions of one of their mascots.

And so it goes. . . .

CHAPTER TWELVE

CHAPTER TWELVE

Following in the (Oversized) Footsteps of a Legend

GROWING UP IN JENKINTOWN, Pennsylvania, Tom Burgoyne's childhood bedroom wasn't much different from the bedrooms of most kids who grew up just a hop, skip, and a jump outside of Philadelphia. There wasn't a piece of wall that wasn't covered up with some sort of Phillies memorabilia or images of Dr. J showcasing his superior dunking ability and "posterizing" yet another embarrassed defender for all of posterity.

Burgoyne, one of six kids, fondly remembers piling into the station wagon with his entire family and heading off to Veterans Stadium to see the Phanatic in action. "We always used to watch the Phanatic," he said. "Even when it was just real basic in the beginning and all he did was run out and knock over the grounds crew and do a little dance to the *Gong Show* song. You definitely didn't go to the bathroom or leave to get popcorn during the fifth inning because you simply had to see what the Phanatic was going to do."

Although the family's seats were typically those of a nosebleed-inducing variety in the stadium's 700 level, Burgoyne recalls one time when he happened to encounter the mascot on the concourse and ended up on the receiving end of a "kiss." "The Phanatic would do this all the time. He'd give somebody a huge smooch and then pretend it was the most disgusting thing that had ever happened to him and proceed to overreact and 'spit it out' and wipe it off," Burgoyne recalls. When the Phanatic kissed him, though, Burgoyne was prepared. He reacted first and "spit it out" himself, copying the moves he had seen the green beast do many times before.

By the time Burgoyne was a senior in high school at St. Joseph's Prep, the satellite school for St. Joseph's University in northwestern Philadelphia, he was happy to be wearing the hawk costume as the school's official mascot. When interviewed by the student paper and asked where he thought he was going to be ten years hence, he didn't really have any clue, but he had to give an answer, so he said, "I'm going to be the Phanatic."

After five years attending nearby Drexel University, Burgoyne's path had gone off in a different direction. He certainly never entertained the idea of being the Drexel Dragon mascot, as he "was spending too much time drinking beer" while enrolled in school. He graduated with a marketing degree and took a job selling business forms and computer supplies. After about seven months of the real world, Burgoyne's daily routine started to incorporate scouring the newspaper classifieds in the hope that something better might come along. One Sunday, it did.

"Mascots wanted: send resume and letter to P.O. Box 7575."

There was nothing to indicate what company had placed the ad, and Burgoyne couldn't be sure this wasn't an offer to dress up as a giant cow and hand out coupons for the local fast-food joint. But he took a chance and sent in an application on a lark. "Two weeks later, I got a call from the Phillies saying they were looking to hire a new Phillie Phanatic," he said. "I was a little confused at first. After all, everyone knew Dave Raymond was the Phanatic. But then they said they were looking for a backup guy to handle a lot of the appearances. So I went in and auditioned."

When he got there, Burgoyne saw that there were about fifteen people competing for the job. He had to interview with a panel that included Raymond, the two costume makers, and the promotions director. He brought with him the article from his high school paper, along with two pictures of him that had made Philadelphia newspapers—one of him celebrating the Phillies' 1980 World Series win atop a statue in Center City and another of him wearing a tuxedo to Julius Erving's final home game. "I wanted to really impress upon them how much of a sports nut I was, and it seemed to work."

Burgoyne then faced a barrage of questions about his personal interests, and he found the line of inquiry quite peculiar. "They were asking me what music do I like to listen to, what are my favorite TV shows, what was my favorite cartoon when I was growing up," he said. "It was like the exact opposite of an IBM interview, where they're trying to weed out the biggest idiot. In this job, they're looking to hire the biggest idiot."

They asked Burgoyne to show off his dance moves right then and there. "The Phanatic does dance—it's a big part of his routine, so if you can't dance, it kind of would have been a deal breaker," he said. "I'm not a great dancer, but I guess I did enough to warrant a callback after lunch and put the costume on."

It seems to me that the request also helped weed out any individuals who might have been too self-conscious to allow themselves to look foolish in front of the panel. If you're going to suffer from stage fright in front of an audience of four or five people, how are you going to react when you have fifty thousand pairs of peepers watching your every move?

After lunch came a "blind audition" in which each candidate got to perform in the costume without the panel knowing who was inside. "They really wanted to be unbiased and judge things based solely on who looked the best in the costume," Burgoyne said. "I remember thinking I was terrible. I was gasping for air. But I left there thinking that even though I wasn't going to get the job, at least I'd have a great story to tell when I got home. You know, 'Hey, guess what? I just got to put on the Phillie Phanatic costume for once in my life.'"

Little did Burgoyne know that it was going to be far more than once. Two weeks later, he received a call telling him he had gotten the job. That was in May of 1989. After about 250 appearances over the course of his first year on the job, he had impressed the organization enough that he was brought on as a full-time employee, working in the phone center for one season before being brought over to the marketing side of things and dealing with promotions. He'd also go up to the control room and help be Dave Raymond's "eye in the sky" when he performed on the field during games.

"In-game entertainment back then wasn't anything like what it is now. We didn't have a CD player until 1992. We still had to use an old cart machine to play funny little sound effects and pop in a cassette tape if Dave's performance called for background music," Burgoyne explained. On some special occasions, Burgoyne would join Raymond on the field, portraying his mom, Phoebe, on Mother's Day, for example. Other times, he'd be the comic foil—taking the full brunt of the mascot's abuse—perhaps by climbing atop the dugout wearing a Mets jersey and getting "stripped naked" to the delight of the home crowd.

In October of 1993, the Phillies went to the World Series, but lost to the Toronto Blue Jays in six games. Still, Burgoyne's spirits were at an all-time high when he got married the following month. But as life-changing an event as a wedding typically is, the process of turning Burgoyne's life upside down was just beginning. While sitting in a bar watching a *Monday Night Football* game in December, Burgoyne couldn't believe his ears. Just before coming back from a commercial break, the local sportscaster came on the screen to tease that night's report and said, "After the game . . . the Phillie Phanatic is retiring. Do you have what it takes to be the Phanatic?"

Burgoyne's jaw hung open. He had already known Raymond was retiring, but couldn't believe that the team was making the news public. He certainly couldn't believe that the team was asking for people to offer up their services to take his place. And in fact, it turned out that this was a case of a newscaster butchering a story by distorting the facts in order to grab the viewer's attention. I know, shocking, right?

"One newscast even went so far as to go to a local school and shove the microphone in kids' faces and ask them how they felt about the Phanatic leaving. These kids were in tears because they thought he was going away. It got out of hand," Burgoyne laments. "We had to put out a press release the next day explaining that while Dave Raymond was leaving, his backup of five years would be taking over and that, yes, at some point we'd probably be looking for a performer to help out, but we're not holding auditions for a new Phanatic at this time."

Nevertheless, Burgoyne chuckled when he recalled that the team received close to 250 résumés and videotapes in the mail over the following few days.

* * *

DEVIN NELSON USED TO THINK that mascots were losers. So when a friend of his asked him to join Team Cosmo—the group of students who manage and perform as the cougar mascot at Brigham Young University—he was more than a little bit skeptical. He wanted nothing to do with it. Two things changed his mind, though: free food and a scholarship.

"After I met the guys involved in the program, I saw they were all actually very athletic, very outgoing, very down to earth—just a good bunch of guys," Nelson said. So he decided to give auditioning a real chance, and after putting on the suit a few times, he realized it wasn't nearly as bad as he had feared. In fact, he quickly discovered how much fun it could be.

"Not all mascot suits are equal. Some just stand there. Some look funny. Some are athletic," Nelson said. "Cosmo the Cougar was athletic and demanded the same athleticism as most professional mascots. I needed to know how to tumble, how to do dunks off a trampoline, and I was encouraged to learn many new skills just in case an opportunity presented itself."

After he graduated from BYU in 2006, an opportunity did present itself—in the form of a gorilla.

The Phoenix Suns had no intention of hiring a mascot back in 1980. It kind of just happened. Henry Rojas was working for a singing telegram company, and he had been sent to Veterans Memorial Coliseum to deliver a message during that night's basketball game.

"I had always been a huge basketball fan and I had told the company that if they ever had a telegram going to a Phoenix Suns game, I wanted to have it. I had seen that done before and I figured I could then stay and watch the rest of the game," Rojas said.

Unfortunately, Rojas lost sight of the usher who had brought him courtside, which was not all that surprising because his vision was somewhat impaired due to the fact that he was dressed head to toe in a gorilla suit—information Rojas wished he had known about sooner.

"I actually tried to get out of it . . . didn't want to do it, but they didn't tell me I was going to be wearing a gorilla suit until it was too late," Rojas said. "The usher had taken the seat number from me and I'm supposed to wait for him to come get me and he never comes back. So I just sat in an empty seat so maybe he would look over and see that there's a gorilla there and he'd remember what he was supposed to do."

However, after waiting for a few minutes Rojas grew antsy, and during the next stoppage in play, he tried to make his way out of the arena as inconspicuously as one can while looking like General Urko from *Planet of the Apes*. That's when the music started to play and, at the urging of a security guard, Rojas went onto the court and began to dance. Tom Ambrose, the Suns' public relations director, immediately got on the phone to try to get rid of this unauthorized intruder, but couldn't get through to anybody, as all eyes were on Rojas.

That's when the magic happened. The crowd responded to the man in the gorilla suit and started to clap along. The antics even amused one of the referees, Ed Rush, who tossed Rojas a basketball. Rojas shot the ball at the basket, it went in, and the crowd roared. The next day, several fans called the team offices saying how much they had enjoyed the gorilla, but by then, Rojas was long gone.

"The next morning, my alarm goes off and the morning radio DJs are talking about it. 'Who was that gorilla who was at the game last night?' It started to create this thing." Rojas said he never just showed up at the Coliseum. He only went when the Eastern Onion Singing Telegram Service got an order and sent him there. Soon, people realized the only way to get the gorilla at the game was to send fictitious telegrams, and so, they did—night after night. Eventually, the local papers started to include a recap of "what the Gorilla did last night" right alongside the Suns' box score.

"Then the Suns asked me to appear at all their playoff games. The Suns wanted *me*. They didn't want Eastern Onion to be able to send just anyone to the game," Rojas said. So at the start of the following season, Rojas signed a one-year, $30,000 contract to appear at all of Phoenix's home games. The year after that, his popularity among the hometown fans had grown so much, he hired an agent to negotiate a new deal and came away with a three-year deal worth more than $100,000.

Rojas's performances started to get so much attention, he was hired by other teams like the Denver Nuggets and the Cleveland Cavaliers to appear at their arenas when the Suns were on a road trip. Nobody in the NBA had ever seen anything like it before. "There were no dancing girls or mascots back then," Rojas said. "When there was a time-out, players would just walk back to their benches. But when I did my thing, even the referees would stop to watch me."

One of those referees was Darell Garretson, who would later go on to be NBA supervisor of officials. Rojas recalls that Garretson had a particular affinity for mascots. "He was the only one who would taunt me on the court before I could taunt him. He'd bring out a banana and try to keep me off-balance and he'd chat with me during the game," Rojas said.

Garretson had served in the US Navy and was stationed in San Diego. He mentioned to Rojas that he had a friend who also was making a career dressed up as an animal—one with feathers. "Garretson wanted to get us together, but Ted did not want us to get together. For some reason, he didn't want to do it," Rojas said. "I think Ted had an issue with me coming in and what I'd become, and I didn't even really know what the Chicken was at the time. It was kind of a competition at that point that I didn't know existed and that I thought was absolutely ridiculous."

Even though Rojas had not heard of the Chicken, he soon found out that the Chicken had heard of him, and according to Rojas, knowing that most people outside of the Phoenix area didn't get much exposure to the Gorilla, Giannoulas was able to poach some of his best material. "He actually stole some bits from me," Rojas said. "I did a bit to the song 'New York, New York.' We put together a special arrangement of the music, trimming it down to a ninety-second bit. I came out with a trench coat and a Frank Sinatra hat and taped a bunch of trash to my leg because there was a sanitation strike in New York [at the time]. The song comes to a climax and I have two guys come out and mug me, steal my watch, my hat, everything. They drag me off the court. And I get a standing ovation. The Knicks players—the time-out is over, but they're clapping and calling for me to take a curtain call. I came back and waved. The next day New York newspapers are slamming me for what I've done. It was great!"

That night, Rojas noticed two guys watching his routine and taking notes. "One of my assistants went over to them and told me they fessed up that they were from the Chicken," he said. "Who knows, maybe they were pulling my leg, but a few weeks later, *he* comes out with a 'New York, New York' bit and I was just like, 'Are you kidding me?'"

Though Rojas was hobnobbing with celebrities and star athletes and making more money than he could have possibly imagined, he found something was missing in his life. "My dad died when I was four. We were very poor. Here's this Hispanic kid who came in the back door of a professional basketball organization. . . . It got so huge, I didn't know how to get out of it," he said. "People loved the Gorilla. You can't just leave."

But Rojas said the job simply did not satisfy him and so, in 1989, he walked away from it all, becoming a motivational speaker in his human form. The Suns were not happy about his decision, and to some extent, he understands why. But he still felt betrayed that on the same day the team was honoring him on the court for all he had done for the organization, they also took out an ad in the local paper looking for his replacement. "That was painful. Where's the sensitivity? I couldn't relate to someone auditioning for something that was mine, that I had created. I know they had thought about just ending it when I had finished, but because of the way I chose to go out, I guess they thought, 'Well, we've already invested in a gorilla—let's see what someone else can do,'" he said.

That someone was Bob Woolf, who added a bit of athletic flair to the act. Woolf had competed as a gymnast at Arizona State University, and now the Gorilla became known for his aerial acrobatics, contorting and flipping through the air in dynamic dunking exhibitions the likes of which had never been seen before. For the next two decades, Woolf would ride motorcycles, jump through rings of fire, and institutionalize the use of a trampoline throughout the NBA's mascot community.

By 2006, the Gorilla was not only doing every single Suns home game throughout the regular season and the seemingly inevitable deep run into the playoffs, but also making more than 250 annual appearances throughout the Valley of the Sun. Woolf, now in his forties, needed a little help keeping up with such a busy schedule.

Devin Nelson told me that when he was hired, he had expected to ease into the job and slowly work his way up to doing the lion's (or gorilla's) share of the performances. According to Nelson, both the Suns and Bob Woolf himself told him that Woolf was going to retire after five more years. The plan was to give Woolf ample time to put his life in order so he could smoothly transition into his next career once he left the suit.

"I didn't know anything about the Gorilla before coming to the Suns. I never understood how big he was, and I had never heard of Bob Woolf," Nelson recalls. He had never planned on becoming a professional mascot, but now he was preparing to fill the shoes of one of the most recognizable characters in all of professional sports.

Nelson watched Woolf in action and shadowed him at some events so he could identify a few moves or actions that he could later, ahem, ape so as not to tip off anyone that a change in performer had taken place. Though Woolf offered up a few pointers during that initial period, Nelson says he didn't share much after that.

"Following the initial appearances I shadowed, he never really gave advice," Nelson said. "From the day I arrived, I felt I was on my own. During my first year, I believe, he treated me like I was there to steal his job and that [he] felt threatened, to the point of occasionally taking his frustration out on me. I ended up learning how to be a professional mascot mostly from the Gorilla's underappreciated game night assistant.

"After my first year, Bob just did his thing and I did mine," Nelson revealed. "Don't get me wrong, he was an amazing mascot and has done amazing things—he just wasn't a good mentor."

Over the next few years, Nelson enjoyed doing a lot of community appearances, relishing those rewarding private moments when there weren't any screaming fans or television cameras around to document things. "Charity events, hospital visits, dying wishes—I saw so many good people doing so many good things for other people," Nelson said. "I always felt blessed to have a job that was so involved with so many good things." Primarily, though, Nelson's job was to do the actual games, along with trips that involved hitting the road and heading out to other NBA arenas, where the Gorilla typically received a hero's welcome. But it wasn't all glory—sometimes, the job warranted hazard pay.

On one occasion, while doing one of his acrobatic dunks, Nelson lost track of where he was in the air and ended up colliding face-first with the rim. "I would have been completely fine, but apparently I stick my tongue out like Michael Jordan and my reflex was to clench my teeth. I bit my tongue, but luckily not all the way through. The doctors stitched me up during the fourth quarter and I had to suck through a straw for the next two weeks."

After three years on the job, Nelson began to realize that Woolf's workload had not lessened at all, as Woolf continued to do most of the outside appearances that came the Gorilla's way. Woolf had not done any post-Gorilla preparation, and apparently the "retirement plan" had been forgotten by management as well. Nelson had not been given any performance reviews by the Suns either, and when he inquired about the possibility of a raise, he was told that the team thought he was already making too much money as it was, even though Nelson says he was making about $15,000 less than the average mascot in the NBA. Of course, if Woolf actually left, that salary gap would have closed considerably.

If Woolf was not planning on making plans for his future, Nelson certainly was not going to make the mistake of standing pat himself. He stuck around for two more seasons before enrolling in school to become a dentist, a profession in which he's still able to put smiles on people's faces, albeit in a much different setting.

"I've seen the Gorilla since leaving the job. It's fun to watch. I miss being a part of everything, but I don't miss putting on the suit," Nelson said.

Just before the end of the 2012 season, Woolf—dressed as the Gorilla—was involved in a fracas at an appearance in Tempe when a Miami Heat fan refused to give Woolf a high five. Woolf reportedly kicked the fan "playfully," which inspired the man to punch the Gorilla in the face, giving him a bloody nose. Both men agreed not to press charges, but the incident still ended up making headlines.

* * *

LUCKILY FOR TOM BURGOYNE, his relationship with Dave Raymond was vastly more collaborative than Devin Nelson's was with Bob Woolf, especially since the changing of the guard in Philadelphia had come with such public fanfare. "In 1994, the *Philadelphia Daily News* put out a list of the fifteen people to watch, and I was at the head of the list, in front of politicians and other bigwigs," Burgoyne said. "I showed up to do my first game and I had reporters at my door telling me they were there to follow me around to see how I did."

Obviously, Burgoyne did just fine, as he can now claim to have been the Phanatic for longer than Raymond. He's only missed four games since he took the job—two of them coming during the first week of the 2008 season due to a minor back injury. Before that he had quite the Ripken-esque streak going, having worked every home game since a series in 1995 when the baseball schedule happened to conflict with the birth of his son. "The team had Phoebe work the game instead and they made an announcement that the Phanatic was busy in the delivery room helping the wife of his 'friend' Tom Burgoyne. As it turns out, the next night, my wife was *still* in labor, so we did the same thing," Burgoyne recalled.

Burgoyne has nothing but good things to say about Raymond. "I think we're very much the same, Dave and I. We have similar, slightly warped senses of humor," he said. "We don't take life too seriously. But I think we can be pretty analytical, pretty grounded, down-to-earth guys when we're not in the costume. And then when we are in the costume, I think it's a free-for-all—common sense being the key element here, and we both have that."

He also echoes Raymond's feeling that the biggest reason for the Phanatic's longevity and continued popularity comes down to the Phillies organization itself. "They have supported the character from day one, and part of that is them giving the performer the freedom to do our own thing and not be looking over our shoulder, not having to run skits by anybody, but just having that trust in us that we're not going do anything inappropriate," Burgoyne said. "Nothing rude or crude. Nothing that is going to delay the game or be a black eye on the team."

Incidentally, Raymond is equally effusive about Burgoyne. "The first time I went to watch the Phanatic and it wasn't me, I thought it was going to be hard to do," Raymond said. "I really did. But Tom is one of the greatest people on the face of the planet and is very talented.

And he still, every chance he gets, says how I gave him an opportunity and how I started this—and he doesn't have to do any of that because he's done such a great job after I left."

● ● ●

WHEN MY TIME WITH THE METS ENDED and Derek Dye was "secretly" hired to take my place, I wasn't afforded the opportunity to play the part of mentor. I'd like to think I would have done so under different circumstances, but as things played out, there was little chance of Derek and I becoming as close as the two Phanatics did.

However, after all this time, my curiosity about how things looked from the other angle was still pretty high, so I tracked Dye down to find out about his perspective on the Mr. Met transition. Suffice it to say, not everything I had been told and believed to be true at the time was accurate.

Dye grew up in Indianapolis and as soon as he graduated high school, he went to Ringling Brothers and Barnum & Bailey Clown College. He wasn't one of the ones chosen to travel with the circus when they took to the road on their next tour, but was tasked with being a "promotional clown"—coming out to help generate local buzz for the show for the one or two appearances when the tour swung through the Indianapolis area. Working just one or two weeks a year was not going to pay the bills, so Dye moved to Cincinnati, where he performed as a freelancer for the zoo and at Kings Island amusement park.

Dye had also hearkened back to the days of Max Patkin by creating a clown character that he took to the Triple-A Indianapolis Indians and got to showcase a few times. That got him interested in the concept of being a mascot. "I was reading a *People* magazine and there was an article about a mascot training course," Dye said. "I was intrigued and so I called up to find out how much it was going to be and when the next openings were. I was quoted some ridiculous price."

One month later, Dye received a return call from the man who ran the course—Dean Schoenewald. He told Dye another magazine was looking to do an article on him and he needed students immediately. He offered to teach Dye for free. "Even though it was free, it was still a scam," Dye said. Apparently, by the time Dye got to the camp, Schoenewald's story had changed.

"He said the Mets had contacted him about a mascot opening, but when I heard that, I just went around him," Dye said. "I think he still ended up milking them for a finder's fee. Dean had a big temper and was not a nice guy. We had so many arguments. He'd kick me out, then beg me to come back. It was crazy."

Leaving Schoenewald behind, Dye proceeded to sell himself to the Mets based on his circus background. He told them he could juggle bats and dance on stilts and ride a unicycle. He sent in a video. "I think they just wanted to see if it could be done," he said. "The interview was at the end of January, but it took forever to get an answer from them. It wasn't until just before I was going to have to move there in March before I found out anything. In the end, I think they hired me more on a dare, just to see if it was possible to do what I said I could do."

So even though Kerry Kaster had told me in the first week of January that he had offered Dye the job, apparently that news didn't make its way back to Dye himself for another two months. This is just par for the course with regard to how the Mets organization operates.

As it turns out, Dye's time in New York was not happy. He moved to the Big Apple in March, went back home to get married during an off week, and moved his new bride to Gotham in May. "It was culture shock," he said. "I grew up on a farm in Indiana. I loved performing and the games were great, but a lot of my memories are tainted by my not being used to or comfortable in New York."

Dye was so unhappy that when he heard about a job opening in Pittsburgh with the Pirates midseason, he fired off his résumé. "There were so many rules and regulations and things I was told not to do. Kerry Kaster would constantly be yelling over the radio for me to stop what I was doing—to get off the dugout, to stop being a distraction to the fans. It was hard to have fun," Dye said. The team had also hired a gaggle of interns dubbed the Pepsi Party Patrol to run around the stadium with the mascot and help create excitement in the stands—an idea Kaster clearly was enamored with after having brought Sports Magic to Shea Stadium twice in 1997.

For Dye, however, all it brought was chaos. The constant disorganization only amplified his feelings of being a fish out of water. Two weeks after the end of the 1998 season, Derek Dye was in Pittsburgh, ready to take over as the full-time Pirate Parrot, filling the opening created when the team let Desi Deceder go. Two weeks after that, Dye heard that Kaster was no longer working for the Mets, either.

In Pittsburgh, Dye had a lot more freedom, though he was warned that there had been issues in the past with the Parrot being "a bit too flirtatious, bordering on sexual harassment." He also found that the Pirates players were much more inclined to goof off with him on the field. In fact, onetime outfielder Brian Giles asked Dye if he could be the Parrot for a bit. "There's a guy making $7 million a year—a professional athlete—running around on the field for fifteen minutes before coming back into the locker room all out of breath, complaining that he can't do it anymore. I was like, 'I have to do this for three hours.' I think he really respected mascots after that," Dye said.

After two seasons, though, Dye and his wife had their first daughter. He heard that the Reds were about to introduce a mascot of their own, so he decided to move back to Cincinnati in the hope that he could land the job with them. Unfortunately, the team was only offering $50 per game, and that wasn't going to buy all the diapers and bottles of formula his child needed. As a result, Dye's mascot career came to an end.

Dye still gets nostalgic about his mascot past. "When I see mascots on TV, the whole experience comes back," he said. "To think that your version of going to the office is something that some people only get to do once a summer. But that's an everyday activity for you. And so to not have that now, it's like, *Wow. Why did I leave? That was so much fun.*"

There wasn't a lot of fun for Dye in 2009, however, when he received a bit of Internet infamy as a result of his new job, in which he visits schools and performs as an "abstinence clown." A video of one of his performances, wherein he showcased his clowning background while offering up bon mots like "Having sex before you are married is just like juggling machetes" and "Sex before marriage will destroy all your life's dreams" went viral and earned the ridicule of certain segments of the blogosphere.

It seems that Parrot curse took a little while to kick in for Dye, but eventually, it found him, too.

❋ ❋ ❋

GENERALLY SPEAKING, THE REPUTATION of Philadelphia sports fans around the country is not all that positive. They've been dealing with the whole "booing Santa Claus" label ever since 1968, when Eagles fans did in fact do just that during a halftime show gone wrong that saw snowballs launched mercilessly at old Kris Kringle.

But given the city's love affair with the Phanatic, perhaps it's time we reconsider how we view sports fans in the City of Brotherly Love. At least that's what Burgoyne thinks should happen. "People don't realize this about Philadelphia. It's got more heart than any city. It really does," he says. "And people never talk about that—heck, I don't talk about that. It's a city of neighborhoods with a lot of heart and a lot of passion, not just for sports, but for everyday life in Philadelphia. The Phanatic can unload a lot of those feelings.

"I think that's something that Dave developed," Burgoyne continued. "He can really be cheering and going crazy one minute, and the next he's flipping somebody off with the tongue or the belly—or he's ticked off, and you can just see his muscles contracting and he's breathing heavy and then he explodes. That emotion—the Phanatic could be part-Italian, he must be from South Philly—expressive. Fans kind of wish they could go on the field or flirt with the pretty blonde in the second row or make fun of the big fat guy coming down the aisle with four cheesesteaks and two popcorns and a couple of sodas."

The Phanatic can and does, and at least for now, so too will Burgoyne. "Somebody else will eventually take my place," he said. "It's a calling. There's always going to be someone who just loves being a mascot and doesn't just want to do it—they *need* to do it. The day that I can't get out of bed anymore after a thirteen-game home stand? Only then will it be time to hang it up."

CHAPTER THIRTEEN

What Lies Ahead
beside the Dying Fire

GETTING A CHANCE TO PLAY in the major leagues is a dream shared by millions of kids all over the country—even the world. So few have the level of talent required to even give the pursuit a realistic go, and even then, the chances of "making the Show" are stacked against even the most capable ballplayers. More than 1,200 players were selected in the 2013 First-Year Player Draft, but less than 10 percent of them will ever get to put on a major league uniform.

Yet, somehow, Adam Greenberg defied all of those odds. In July of 2005, three years after being selected by the Chicago Cubs in the ninth round of that year's draft, and after toiling through stops in Lansing, Michigan; Dayton, Florida; Jackson, Tennessee; and Des Moines, Iowa, he got the call that every player waits his whole life for—he was going to the Show.

His family came to witness the culmination of all of Greenberg's hard work as the Cubs battled the Marlins in Florida, but he didn't see any game action during his first day with the team. After riding the pine for eight innings the following day, Greenberg was sent to the plate to pinch-hit for pitcher Will Ohman in the ninth. It was finally happening.

One pitch later, Greenberg was lying on the ground.

The pitch by Valerio de los Santos—a ninety-two-mile-per-hour fastball—had hit Greenberg in the back of the head, and even though he was wearing a protective helmet, the damage was done. Greenberg was helped from the field by trainers, and due to the postconcussion symptoms that lingered long after that one pitch, he was unable to play again in 2005.

Over the next few years, Greenberg bounced around from organization to organization, trying to latch on somewhere and earn a return to the major leagues, but he never seemed to gain much traction. But in 2012, Greenberg's cause was picked up by a die-hard Cubs fan and documentary filmmaker named Matt Liston.

Liston was watching the film *Field of Dreams* with his wife when she said she felt sorry for a character named Moonlight Graham, based on a real-life player who played in just one major league game in 1905 but never got a chance to swing the bat. That prompted Liston to recall the story of Greenberg. When he discovered that Greenberg was still playing, Liston reached out to him and said he wanted to help him get that "one at-bat."

Liston started an online petition to help spread the word about Greenberg's quest and then set out to see if he could make it a reality. "I spoke with the owner of the Cubs before the season started at a banquet and he seemed open to the idea," Liston told me. "In May, I talked to Jed Hoyer (the general manager of the Cubs) and he seemed open to the idea as well, but said it would be tough."

As time went on, and the end of the season grew closer, Liston found that the team was no longer returning his calls. However, the media buzz surrounding the possibility of Greenberg getting another chance was snowballing, prompting the Cubs to release a statement. They said no.

The Miami Marlins, however, said yes. Whether it was guilt over their team's involvement in Greenberg's injury or simply a way of trying to generate some positive publicity for a baseball team that had not played up to expectations, Marlins president David Samson called Liston and said he wanted to meet.

"The Mets were playing the Marlins in New York's last home series of the year, and I got a call to meet with Samson. He said he wanted to do this, but would leave the ultimate decision up to the commissioner. I thought it would take maybe two weeks to get approval, but it took only minutes—one phone call. Bud Selig knew all about our campaign, he knew why we were calling him, and he was all for it," Liston said, still amazed by how quickly the pieces fell into place.

Greenberg was allowed to sign a one-day contract with the Miami Marlins and would be given the chance to pinch-hit in a game—in Miami—against the New York Mets on October 2, 2012. I asked Liston if the Mets organization had to sign off on this at all, and he said no. "Selig was the only person who had to approve, and he did. Out of courtesy, we asked—and the truth is, it was a bit of a madhouse with all the buildup to Adam's at-bat. It totally affected the Mets. They were mobbed with questions, especially R. A. Dickey (the pitcher who would face Greenberg) and David Wright (who also had been hit in the head by a pitch). But they were all classy, and Adam found a team-signed bat from the Mets in his locker."

* * *

WHEN ISAIAH ARPINO WAS GROWING UP in Altoona, Pennsylvania, he would always look forward to going to games at the local baseball stadium. It wasn't so much that he was a fan of the Altoona Curve, the minor league baseball team that played there, as it was that he was simply enthralled by the mascots, to the point of following them around the stadium.

Oftentimes, one of the characters he'd tail like a bloodhound was Reggy the Purple Party Dude, a friendly, furry face with french fries for hair that was created and originally performed by none other than Dave Raymond. Reggy would tour minor league stadiums around the country and made occasional stops in Altoona.

When Arpino was fifteen or so, he had a chance encounter with the man who regularly performed as Steamer, the Curve's mascot, who offered Arpino a chance to shadow him. Apparently, he was ready to move on after a decade or so of playing Steamer, and it wasn't long before the baton was handed off.

Arpino was incredibly gung ho about his good fortune, but wanted to make sure he didn't screw up his chance, so he decided to attend Dave Raymond's Mascot Boot Camp, held annually on the campus of Kutztown University in eastern Pennsylvania, to learn the tricks of the trade.

Arpino took to mascotting like a fish to water. Raymond was so impressed that he hired him to be a backup for new characters that were being created by his company. Arpino also caught the eye of university staff as well, and they offered him the opportunity to be the school's mascot—a big golden bear named Avalanche—if he decided to attend the school as a freshman in the fall.

He accepted the offer and has been doing all three jobs ever since. At some point down the road, he might well find himself being promoted to "game squire" for Reggy's summer tour—in essence, being part bodyguard, part roadie, and part comic foil for the character, but that's still up in the air.

On this particular Saturday in March of 2013, however, Arpino sits in the back of a meeting room in the Student Recreation Center on the Kutztown campus. Boot camp is once again in session, and Dave Raymond has graciously allowed me to witness the day's proceedings as a fly on the wall. I'm looking forward to seeing what the next generation of mascots looks like and how they feel about the job.

When I arrive, class is already under way, and there's nary a costume in sight. Dave Raymond, wearing a visor and a bright yellow shirt, greets me warmly before returning to grade his nine students on the pop quiz he'd just administered. This test was all about "fun" and goes to the heart of Raymond's philosophy—that there is power in having fun and that it's essential to stop the fun-killers from winning the day.

His grading of the exam is quite lenient. In fact, most of the answers are still clearly visible in black magic marker on the large sheets of paper that hang around the front of the room. Raymond simply wants his charges to begin to internalize the lessons of the day: the core components of being a mascot include movement and dance, nonverbal skills, ample practice time, and setting aside time to be creative.

Raymond emphasizes that if you want to avoid being thought of as "just a kid in a suit," you have to become a performer. You need to be cognizant of things like proper nutrition and the biology of sweating so you can always be at your best while in costume. However, a cursory glance around the room reveals that Dave and I are the only ones who are out of our twenties. These *are* just kids, and each of them has a different reason for being there.

Josh is the mascot for the Rochester Red Wings, the Triple-A affiliate of the Baltimore Orioles, and is clearly the most experienced of all the camp's participants. He's spent two years performing as Spikes, a roosterlike bird, for the minor league baseball team while also doubling as the catering sales manager for the team. He can see himself doing the job until he no longer enjoys it, and he's happy where he is right now and doesn't see the gig as a stepping-stone to the major leagues by any means.

John is from a local high school, and he's more interested in moving to either New York or Los Angeles to try to make it as an actor or voice-over artist than he is in being a mascot. However, he says he'd love to leave his school's program better off than it was when he inherited it.

Some of the other performers are from nearby universities, including Greg and Eric, both of whom rotate into the furry form of Avalanche at Kutztown along with Isaiah Arpino, while Tom hails from Gwynedd-Mercy College, located just northwest of Philadelphia. Tom's outfit is by far the most restrictive of the bunch, as his griffin suit—which bears a strong resemblance to Sam the Eagle of the Muppets—has a long, stiff head that comes attached to a shoulder harness and quite significantly restricts his ability to move.

Central Connecticut State has sent both of their Blue Devil performers for the intensive weekend. Zack really wants to learn how to not burn out after just a few minutes in the suit. He's there with Charlie, who saw Zack performing in the costume during her first week of school as a freshman and immediately decided there was nothing else she'd rather do. Although she is the first female to try out as the school's mascot, she says there was absolutely no resistance. "Really, I think it's as simple as that no girl ever expressed an interest before me," she says.

Most of the attendees have been sent by their organizations, with the school or team picking up the tab. That's why Travis is here all the way from Georgia. He certainly wouldn't have come on his own, as he originally was "forced" to take on the role of Chopper, the groundhog mascot for Georgia's Gwinnett Braves, the Triple-A affiliate of the Atlanta Braves. But he does admit that even though there was a lot of arm-twisting to get him inside the suit that first time, he was hooked once he witnessed "that first kid who was terrified of the suit who by the end of the game was suddenly hugging Chopper and sad for him to leave."

The least-experienced member of the group, though, is Ryan. He is representing Skylands Ice World and is stepping into a mascot costume—in the form of some kind of an abominable snowman—for the very first time. He looks a bit out of place in this group, and in fact in this decade, as his long hair makes him look like an extra from *Dazed and Confused*. At twenty years of age, Ryan says he took this "out-of-the-box job" so he wouldn't have to be a machinist and miserable. "I'd rather be poor and happy," he surmises.

Truth be told, a lot—if not all—of the work that goes into becoming a top-notch mascot comes when you're outside of the suit. Being able to recognize a good idea and develop it and craft it into something that can entertain a crowd takes a lot of time and effort. You can't expect to go on the court without ever having picked up a basketball—even if you're taller than Manute Bol—and think you're going to be successful going up against LeBron James. So why would anyone think grabbing Jimmy the Intern and stuffing him into a mascot suit, likely (as in the case of Travis) against his will, is going to end well?

With the arrival of one last, special student, the group gets ready to unzip their behemoth duffel bags and take out the menagerie of beasts ensconced within. That special student is Shea Humphrey, all of nine years old. He's a huge sports fan and has gained a bit of notoriety in his hometown of Pelham, New York, where he is a frequent attendee at as many local high school sporting events as he can get himself to.

When he's in the stands, he jumps to his feet and gets the crowd riled up with his exuberant cheerleading. He doesn't even have to wear a costume in order to be considered the de facto mascot of the school. Shea is slightly developmentally delayed, but funny and full of spirit and such a big fan of mascots that when Dave Raymond was forwarded some video of the kid in action along with a request for him to attend the camp, it was nigh on impossible to decline.

As each performer dons his or her head, Shea squeals with glee and puts on his own Transformers mask so that he, too, can take part in the training. He also becomes glued at the hip to Chopper, and it is clear by observing the interaction of the pair that Travis wasn't kidding when he told me that dealing with kids is his favorite part of the job.

Raymond takes the gang through "professional idiot" training exercises, where looking foolish is to be admired, rather than something to be embarrassed about. First comes "head dancing," followed by a series of improvisational exercises aimed at getting the performers used to communicating without words. Raymond tells me his mother was deaf and that she would sometimes turn off her hearing aid at the height of an argument, so very early on in life he had to learn how to make his points silently.

Next, the group sheds their heads and returns to their desks for an exercise in group dynamics and a lesson on brainstorming. Raymond splits the students into groups of three and challenges them to come up with a plan to save the *Titanic*. They have ten minutes to work together to figure out, assuming the ship does hit the iceberg and begins to sink, how to save all of the passengers without resorting to impossible things like time travel or alien spaceships coming to their rescue. Then, the teams will share their ideas with each other.

Raymond's goal is to demonstrate that there are no bad ideas. Rather than saying "That won't work" and being negative about the ideas you don't like, the key to successful brainstorming is to simply select the ideas you like best without having to denigrate the ones you think might be foolish. This helps to foster an atmosphere where people aren't afraid to think well outside the box—and, in fact, it's exactly those kinds of crazy and outlandish ideas from which the best results often spring.

When one participant postulates that perhaps "a boat containing a clown convention happens to sail by the *Titanic* as it's sinking and they happen to have an unlimited supply of balloons," the entire room can't help but break into laughter. However, the ludicrous image does seem to spark the notion that perhaps there's a realistic way to increase the amount of buoyant surface available to the passengers, and *that's* a thought that could ultimately lead to a winning strategy.

The reason Raymond wants them to learn how to support even the most outlandish ideas is that at the end of camp on Sunday, each trio will be tasked with performing a two-minute skit. They'll be provided with a large cardboard box, a tablecloth, and a choice of one additional prop they find lying around the facility. Their music will be selected for them, but other than that, they can do pretty much whatever they want in order to entertain an audience of volunteers who will be on hand to witness the promised zaniness.

Raymond tells me confidentially that the results of this exercise are beside the point. "Most of them *will* totally suck, and they'll see it as a failure. But it's a lesson in how much they have to do. Of course they failed—there's not enough time. But in reality, they won't have skits handed to them, they won't have props lying around—they'll need to construct them. They are going to be on their own, but hopefully I've given them the skills to develop winning skits down the line."

*   *   *

WHEN MOST PEOPLE ARE asked what the most important part of a mascot's job is, the answer is usually related to entertaining the crowd. But it's not. The truth is, teams have mascots in order to make money. Be it through merchandising the character or simply having fans enjoy the mascot enough that it encourages them to frequent the ballpark time and time again, at the end of the day, business is business.

A mascot performer might be the most creative person in the world when it comes to creating skits. He might have dance moves that would make Gene Kelly and Fred Astaire jealous. But the key to keeping your job as a mascot comes on the marketing end of things. Certainly you're going to want to have a funny idea, but the trick to longevity isn't just creating a really clever spin on a game of tug-of-war. It's about using that skit to court a local gym or towing company to pay the team for the right to add their name to the mix. All of that comes only after a performer already has a job to begin with, though. The difficult part is getting your foot in the door—and when it comes to mascots, those feet can be pretty big.

After a break for lunch, Raymond gets all the performers into full costume for only the second time all weekend. The previous night, all of them had suited up for a minor league hockey game at the nearby Lehigh Center, where they helped the Reading Royals—a Washington Capitals affiliate—celebrate the birthday of their team's mascot, Slapshot. Between periods, it was sheer pandemonium as close to forty mascots of all shapes and sizes took to the ice.

Attendees ranged from the recognizable Swoop of the Philadelphia Eagles and the Penn State Nittany Lion to the less familiar Sonic soda cup and other amorphous blobs representing local businesses. They tossed T-shirts into the crowd to the "music" of Ke$ha, but it was too chaotic for Raymond to be able to provide any meaningful feedback.

But now Raymond's boot camp goes into full-on drill mode, with performers being asked to dance, exercise, display varying levels of emotion, walk across the room with a purpose and an attitude, and all kinds of assorted wackiness. Just being able to see other people in action, sharing similar experiences, and watching how other performers apply constructive criticism on the spot can't help but make these performers better. Even in such a short period of time, I can see some of them becoming far more self-aware and self-confident.

I'm particularly tickled by how well Charlie is doing. Because her school sent only one costume, Zack was the one who got to perform as the Blue Devil. Charlie was wearing a second costume sent along by the Rochester Red Wings—Mittsy, the female counterpart to Spikes. Although this character was completely foreign to her, Charlie immediately imbued it with such personality, it's easy to see that she's not deluding herself when she tells me she thinks about doing this professionally one day.

The last thing on the agenda before the performers break off into groups to brainstorm skit ideas is a "simulated live mascot audition." Raymond plays the part of an interviewer and, dressed as Avalanche, Isaiah Arpino attempts to set himself apart from the rest of the competition and earn himself a job.

From the moment he enters the room, Arpino is in character, responding to Raymond's every question with gigantic flourishes of his arms. His energy level is incredibly high as Raymond asks him to perform many of the drills that the boot camp attendees have just gone through themselves, and they are rapt with attention. By the time Arpino has finished off a series of dances set to a medley of music ranging from big band to rap, country to classic rock, the students are all applauding and cheering wildly.

The enthusiasm level in the room has skyrocketed, and while most of the attendees are only now beginning to realize how far they have to go to get to Arpino's level of expertise—and perhaps are a little bit scared by the size of that gap—they're also encouraged and reassured by the fact that Arpino was sitting right where they are only a few short years ago.

While most auditions do take on a form that resembles the simulation observed by Dave Raymond's boot campers in Kutztown, one never knows for sure exactly what shape a mascot search is going to take. In 2012, the Houston Astros were playing in their last season in the National League before moving the franchise over to the American League in order to balance out the number of teams in each league. When they also learned that the performer who had portrayed Junction Jack had decided to call it a career, the team decided that they would simply retire the character as well.

So they held an open casting call and solicited applications from anyone who wanted a chance to become Orbit, a green space alien that had actually been the team's mascot in the final years of their stay at the Astrodome. Greg Cirrone, who had been toiling as a hockey mascot at the minor league level, was one of the few out-of-towners contacted by the team.

He was actually attending a Boston Red Sox game on a Friday night at Fenway Park when he received an e-mail. "If I wanted to audition, I needed to be in Houston on Tuesday. It was very short notice, and I wasn't sure it was worth it to spend the money on a plane ticket to go out there, but in the end I decided to go," Cirrone said.

Cirrone arrived just in time for a face-to-face interview that narrowed down the field of applicants from fifty to ten. After an overnight stay at a budget hotel, he returned to the stadium to perform a one-minute skit, no music or talking allowed. "They rented each of us a $20 polar bear costume from a Halloween costume store and threw us each out there for ten minutes to interact with fans and do our minute-long skit. It was tough to work out of and uncomfortable."

After that, Orbit's fate was put in the hands of Internet voting. Yes, the decision on which of the ten finalists would get to advance to the final four would be determined, at least in part, in *Dancing with the Stars* fashion. Videos of each performer were posted online, and the ones that received the most votes would survive the cut. While the team was sure to point out that only a portion of each candidate's final score would be influenced by fan vote, it certainly didn't hurt that some contestants had created Facebook fan pages to drum up support for their own campaigns.

After two weeks of sweating it out, Cirrone says he got an e-mail from the team informing him that he had not made it to the final four. He was disappointed, especially after he learned that the eventual winner of the competition, Richard Tapia, was already an employee of the team, having worked as an account executive for group sales.

Tapia had a mascot background, first at the University of Texas and later on with the Astros' Triple-A affiliate in Round Rock, Texas, and likely deserved the victory, but Cirrone has his doubts. "Ultimately, it's their organization and they have the right to pick who they want. But finding out Richard already worked there—I'm not saying it was rigged, but it makes you think," Cirrone mused.

I did contact Tapia to see if he would discuss the competition from his point of view, but as I expected, he said the team frowns upon his giving interviews, as they'd prefer he maintain a low public profile. He would, however, offer the following statement: "It's definitely been a long road from high school, college, minor leagues, and now to being here. I'm really looking forward to this opportunity and seeing where things go."

Cirrone continues to make cold calls to teams across the country and scours the want ads in the hopes of catching that big break. However, he is well aware that the window of opportunity is a small one and that the clock is ticking. "I guess I can only realistically look a couple of more years without getting a break," he says. "But there are no guarantees in life."

Well, maybe just one: Cirrone promises he will not be watching any Astros games in the future. I can't say I blame him.

Before I leave boot camp, I catch up with Arpino and ask him what *he* thought of his performance during Raymond's mock audition. Performers are typically their own worst critics, so I'm not surprised that he's already picking it apart in his head. He's unhappy that he suddenly lost steam at one point—it was indeed apparent to me that he'd hit the wall during the second song of the dance medley—but I tell him I didn't think anybody but Dave and I even noticed. We've both definitely been there, so we can see the subtle signs that most people would miss.

In truth, Arpino is already a better mascot than I ever was or could have hoped to be. Whether he ultimately chooses to work in Major League Baseball or the NBA, I have no doubt that he will have a very long career in this business once he finishes his time at Kutztown University.

✸ ✸ ✸

ON OCTOBER 2, 2012, Adam Greenberg finally got an official at-bat in a Major League Baseball game. He received a standing ovation as he walked to the plate in the sixth inning to face the dancing knuckleball of R. A. Dickey. Three pitches later, all strikes, Greenberg walked back to the dugout, again to thunderous applause. In spite of the result, he couldn't have been happier to get that second chance.

As Liston told me, his biggest fear was that Greenberg would walk, which, due to baseball's rules, would not have counted as an official at-bat. "Adam is tough. He's an elite athlete," Liston said. "This was more than a publicity stunt. This wasn't a contest winner or something. Adam Greenberg was—and is—a baseball player. When you see him, he's in crazy shape. Quite frankly, if he had walked, I bet he would have stolen second base."

So what does Adam Greenberg's story have to do with mine?

Well, when I first heard about Greenberg's quest, I couldn't help but laugh to myself about the irony of the New York Mets being so behind his return to the majors. I mean, they could have raised a stink about the stunt being an affront to the "integrity of the sport." In fact, when I spoke to Liston, he said he was surprised there wasn't more blowback and comparison to the infamous Eddie Gaedel incident of 1951, when Bill Veeck—the same man who gave Max Patkin his start at baseball clowning—sent the über-diminutive three-foot-seven Gaedel up to bat wearing uniform number $\frac{1}{8}$. Gaedel walked on four pitches to the cheers and laughter of the home crowd.

Gaedel's walk, like Greenberg's hit-by-pitch, did not count as an official at-bat and after the game, outrage from the league and a change in the procedures regarding the preapproval of contract signings ensured that there would be no repeat of Veeck's shenanigans. Never again would a team's mascot—which is pretty much what Gaedel's association with the team had been—be allowed to actually take part in the game itself.

Shortly after I had decided to return to the mascot world for one last hurrah, I had contacted the Mets about the possibility of getting in the Mr. Met costume again. Every road led to the same conclusion. The fate of my request laid in the hands of the one man who made all of the decisions regarding Mr. Met. That man was Tim Gunkel. Just as he had in 1997 when he denied my request for health insurance, Gunkel still held all of the cards in determining if I ever would get back inside the giant smiling baseball head again.

Gunkel sent me an e-mail that, although cordial in tone and complete with an offer for me and my family to come to a game and watch from the stands whenever I wanted, included the following denial of my request: "I understand the reason for your request, and I am sorry to disappoint [you] but this isn't something we can do. We treat Mr. Met like the icon he is, and we don't put people in the costume for stunts, media attention, etc. We've had plenty of requests, including some like this that are harder to turn down. But we have been consistent in our respect for this tradition. With your background as a mascot performer, I am sure you understand."

When I read the reply to Liston, he couldn't believe it. "That's just not right, man," he said, as perplexed by the resistance as I was. And yet, given my prior experience with the Mets organization, I couldn't say I was surprised. Although I had anticipated a rejection, it was the part about respect for tradition that rankled me.

The whole point of my attempting this journey was to see how much of the personality I had created as Mr. Met had endured. I certainly didn't feel like a "guest performer" because I truly believe that once you have been in the costume, not only are you a permanent part of Mr. Met, but he is also permanently a part of you.

Respect for tradition? When the Mets closed down Shea Stadium and had a big ceremony after the final game of the 2008 season, the team invited back former players, broadcasters, stadium staff—all of whom were given one last chance to say goodbye. You know who didn't get a call? Me—or anyone else who had worn the costume after I left. Apparently, treating Mr. Met "like the icon he is" doesn't include any acknowledgment of the people who helped create (or to preserve) that iconic status in the first place.

Clearly, Gunkel does not see the contradiction in his saying that the tradition of Mr. Met would be damaged if they let "just anybody" in the suit while at the same time refusing to recognize that, in this particular instance, I'm not just anybody.

Contrast this attitude with how the Philadelphia Phillies treat Dave Raymond. "I still live vicariously through the Phanatic,"

Raymond says. "And whatever he does, even a World Series parade, the Phillies have always been very nice to me and invited me back to most all of these types of events. When the Phanatic's costume was put in the Hall of Fame, they brought me and my son up there and paid for the whole trip. They've been more than gracious, and that's made it extremely easy to step back and watch it grow."

I'm not suggesting that my contribution to the legacy of Mr. Met is as significant as Raymond's was to the Phanatic, and I certainly never had the kind of relationship with the Mets that he's had with the Phillies, but if I sound bitter—I can't and won't deny that I did (and do) feel that way—I felt even worse after having shared some of these feelings in a follow-up e-mail to Gunkel that got no response. In fact, all of my further attempts to contact him or to go above his head within the organization were rebuffed.

Time heals all wounds, but only if you're aware of those wounds to begin with. It wasn't until I embarked on this mascot journey that I realized I hadn't let it go. I've been carrying this bitterness around with me all this time.

When it comes to mascot performers, this is the inevitable place the vast majority of us end up, in spite of our best efforts to remember only the happy times and to forget about the times our contributions were trivialized away by the unfeeling zombies we had to work with—or more often, around—on a daily basis.

So there would be no deus ex machina to save the day, no joy in Mr. Met-ville for me. No happy reunion with my bigheaded alter ego, no rally in the final at-bat, no ball miraculously rolling through Bill Buckner's legs. Like many of my comrades in costume and friends in fur before me, this is how my mascot career ends. On somebody else's terms.

CHAPTER FOURTEEN

The Happy Recap

IN JULY OF 1995, I came back into my locker room at Shea Stadium after a particularly exhausting stint in the Mr. Met costume, drenched in sweat and running on fumes, only to discover that while I had been away, someone had stolen my wallet. At the time, the only thing standing between the privacy of my changing area and the influx of thousands of fans entering the stadium through Gate D was a single door secured by an ancient deadbolt lock and hinges that were barely hanging on for dear life. Every employee in the stadium not only had a key to this door since the room also housed the "employee gym," but most of them also would forget to lock the door behind them when they left—especially on game days.

Nobody at the stadium showed any concern or offered me any assistance, so by the time I called police to report the incident—and you try explaining to an officer that you were on the field at Shea Stadium at the time your wallet was stolen and get taken seriously—the thief had already managed to charge goods worth several thousand dollars to my credit cards at various stores located one subway stop away. In the end, the incident didn't end up costing me anything, save the nuisance of having to replace my driver's license and everything else that was in the wallet. Eventually the team gave me another line of defense—a second door behind which I could feel a bit more secure locking up my personal valuables when I was in the Mr. Met suit, and lock up Mr. Met himself when I wasn't.

I had not heard of this incident until recently, but apparently, in

May of 1998, the season after I left, Mr. Met was stolen. Having not learned their lesson, the Mets moved the headquarters for the mascot and the Pepsi Prize Patrol out behind the right-field bullpen, into an area that was separated from the vast stadium parking lot by a single chain-link fence.

Thieves apparently hopped the fence, lifted up the flimsy garage door used to secure the location, and stole baseball bats, T-shirts, some walkie-talkies, Derek Dye's unicycle, and the Mr. Met costume itself, giant head and all. The team's official comment on the incident, as reported by a local Queens newspaper, read as follows: "Mets officials said that Mr. Met was devastated when he walked into his office and found his uniform gone."

There's so much wrong about this story that I don't know where to begin. But then again, as I was once told to put Mr. Met's head inside a large garbage bag and hold it in my lap as I rode a Greyhound bus to the All-Star Game in Philadelphia, I am not surprised in the least. Nor am I surprised that, even with the Mets organization's inept attempts to build their mascot program, Mr. Met remains just as popular today, if not more so, as he was when I first tightened the wing nuts on that polyurethane shell so many years ago.

Mascots create characters that can't help but become bigger than the teams they represent. Players come and go. Management gets fired and new ownership takes over. And yes, as I've learned all too well from firsthand experience, the performer inside the suit far too frequently gets tossed aside without receiving any gratitude for a job well done. Yet the mascot lives on—and with every smiling child who comes to the ballpark and stares in wide-eyed wonder at the costumed creature cheering for the home team, their power grows to the point where nothing short of killing the character will slow its surging popularity or cut into its longevity.

* * *

IN MAY OF 2012, Dean Schoenewald's name popped up in the *Press of Atlantic City* in an article about the growing crime rate in the casino resort town. He told police that he and his family had returned home from dining out to find three men with guns waiting for them. Schoenewald said that one of them had held a gun to his daughter's head and a second one had chased his seven-year-old son down the street while he fought *mano a mano* with the third until the gun accidentally discharged in the fracas.

Schoenewald said he pretended to have gotten shot, and that lie was enough to cause all three men to flee without further incident. He claimed the men were there in retaliation for his snitching to the police about a local drug dealer, and said he and his family would be relocating to a new town he would not reveal for fear of a repeat attack.

Perhaps that's why it was a bit surprising to see Schoenewald on television one month later, having called up local media outlets to get publicity for a Flag Day stunt he was performing. Schoenewald took to a vacant lot in Atlantic City to burn a dozen American flags in order to spread the word about preserving "the ideology of freedom." Even forgetting for a moment the outlandishness and controversy of his actions, one has to wonder why a man who had had to move his family just a month before for fear of being found was suddenly calling up reporters so they could broadcast his whereabouts to anyone who happened to turn on their television set.

In truth, since leaving the mascot world behind, Schoenewald has been accused of—by his own count—652 crimes, including drug running, human trafficking, and running fraudulent charities. When Philadelphia's local NBC affiliate reported on Schoenewald's

Up to Par Foundation and suggested that bucketfuls of donations collected from drivers stopped at traffic lights were in fact filling Schoenewald's pockets, he attempted to sue the station for a hundred million dollars.

Since his bout of public pyromania, Schoenewald has apparently been laying low, but I'm certain that before too long, the man who once tried to start up a women's football league in Colorado and held down several stints as a Christian radio host will find the need for attention too great to resist and will again end up in the eye of some storm of his own creation. Once you've been on the receiving end of the cheers of a huge crowd, it's hard to go back to being just one anonymous face in it.

* * *

WHEN WE LAST LEFT Nick Natario, he was torn. Should he continue to pursue his dream of being a professional mascot, or leave that world behind and shoot for a career in journalism instead? Ultimately, he opted to go to that audition for the Connecticut Sun and this time, when the final decision ended up being between Natario and another former Raymond trainee, things did go Natario's way.

"They offered me the job and I turned it down," Natario says. "I had just interviewed at a television station in Elmira, and even though they hadn't given me an answer yet, I had a really good feeling about that, so I said thanks, but no thanks. It was tough."

Natario's gut feeling paid off. He got the job and worked as a reporter in upstate New York for two years before moving to Burlington, Vermont, in May of 2011. His career took off at Fox 44 News as a multimedia journalist, features reporter, and all-around one-man band. You might see him reporting serious news stories concerning the latest Vermont court proceedings, but more often than not, Natario's assignments end up with him engaged in such things as making snow angels during a feature piece after a blizzard or spending a night in a haunted house to see what ghosts happen by. Clearly, he's having a blast.

"I actually do use a lot of my mascot background in my work," Natario says. "I know I made the right choice. I even got to do a piece where we shared our 'hidden talents' and I got into a mascot costume again for the first time in years. I had fun doing it—for a day."

Natario does sometimes get a bit nostalgic for his mascot roots when he's watching live sporting events, but sometimes bitterness does manage to creep in. "The way it ended with Dave Raymond left a sour taste in my mouth that all these years later is still there," he says. "I really wanted to be a mascot for a major league team and I never thought I would be punished for trying to pursue my dreams."

He has talked to Raymond a few times over the years, though not often. And while the two are never going to be best buddies, Natario doesn't equivocate when it comes to Raymond's body of work. "For high school or college kids who want to be a mascot? I still recommend going to his boot camp and watching him and learning what he has to offer. He is the best at what he does," Natario says. "He is the man to know."

In the end, for Natario, it comes down to being happy with his choices. "I love what I do now," he says. "I really do. I still get to have fun and goof around, the only difference being that now I have to go to the gym because you can actually see what I look like."

And if a major league team picked up the phone tomorrow and offered Natario a job?

"I would happily decline."

* * *

ON NOVEMBER 1, 2013, fans at Denver's Pepsi Arena looked on in horror as the seemingly lifeless form of Rocky, the Denver Nuggets mountain lion mascot, was slowly lowered to the court from the rafters where he had been hanging from a harness while waiting to make his grand entrance at the team's home opener.

According to Denver's ABC affiliate, team officials said Rocky only "had the wind knocked out of him" and that he eventually walked off under his own power, but video of the incident certainly made it appear that the mascot had suffered a far worse—and vastly more permanent—fate. Thankfully, it looks like Rocky dodged a major bullet.

Three weeks later, while rehearsing a stunt prior to the Kansas City Chiefs' November 24th game against the San Diego Chargers, Dan Meers was not as lucky. Dressed as KC Wolf, Meers was practicing a descent from the top of Arrowhead Stadium to the field below via a zipline when, according to attorney Tim Dollar, a malfunction in the rigging caused him to plummet into the upper deck seats instead.

Meers reportedly suffered a broken back, ribs, and tailbone along with a collapsed lung and underwent major surgery in order to repair the damage. After two weeks spent at a local hospital, Meers was allowed to return home to continue his long road to recovery.

Less than a week after Meers's accident, Michaela Mills, the Mississippi State student inside the football team's Bulldog costume, was reportedly struck by a camera cart covering the game for television. The result, according to Scott Strickland, the school's athletic director, was a broken leg.

To her credit, she kept her costume's head on the entire time that the medical team was treating her injury and stayed in character even while being carted off on a stretcher. Two surgeries later, it appears that Mills will ultimately be fine.

As for Meers, one can only hope that he, too, will be able to get back to full health and that his mascot career hasn't come to a premature end, but it only goes to show how dangerous this job can sometimes be—and incidents like these, while rare, still happen far too frequently.

KC Wolf, on the other hand, did not miss a game.

* * *

THERE'S AN OLD SCIENCE-FICTION MOVIE called *Logan's Run* about a futuristic society in which overpopulation has gotten so out of control that the only way to prevent resources from running out is to euthanize everyone when they reach their thirtieth birthdays. They achieve this at a ceremony called Carrousel, a bizarre Cirque du Soleil piece of performance art that ends up not with presents and cake, but with all of the participants getting incinerated into oblivion while hordes of onlookers cheer with reckless abandon.

That's kind of what the mascot world feels like to me now. My time has come and gone, while Mr. Met and his cohorts on the diamond, ice, court, gridiron, pitch, and everywhere else games are played will continue to live on, their performers getting "renewed" as the current occupants reach their expiration dates.

If my journey has taught me anything, it's that the future is in good hands—be it Max Woerner, who continues to grow as a performer while cheering on his Ocean City Nor'easters, or Charlie Williams, who is well on her way to making sure that the pro ranks don't revert back to an all-boys club. And I'm genuinely excited to see where Isaiah Arpino ends up. Whatever team's fans get to enjoy his exploits on a regular basis are in for a huge treat, even if they never end up knowing his name.

As for me, I've found the best kind of closure in the form of my son, Xander, who was right there with me on this journey, sitting in the stands when I walked around as both Bobby and Buster. Being able to see the wonder in his eyes as he watched me transform into those characters and put smiles on the faces of so many people made me feel extremely grateful for the experience.

In October, when the time came for Xander to decide what he wanted to be for Halloween, he didn't hesitate in choosing a costume. Armed with papier-mâché, paint, and the help of an incredibly artistic mother, Xander went trick-or-treating as Mr. Met. Maybe the Mets were unwilling to give me one last chance to say goodbye to the character I helped shape and develop during my four years with the organization, but it no longer mattered to me. As I watched the person I continue to help shape and develop each and every day running from door to door with his friends, laughing away and enjoying life, there was no longer any reason to hold on to the past.

* * *

HENRY ROJAS LEFT THE PHOENIX SUNS at a time when most people thought he was crazy to do so. Since that time, he has served as a pastor and counselor and uses his voice—something he never used while in costume as the Gorilla—to try to motivate students to become better people.

He does not for a single minute regret his decision. "It was awesome to walk away from it and never have to wear the mask again," he says. "I never regret not wearing the mask because I always felt trapped. I hated getting ready for personal appearances and putting the black makeup on, putting on the costume, and sweating like a dog. After I began to do public speaking, I found the joy of being able to stand up there, make people laugh, entertain, and most importantly, not have to take a shower afterward."

All jokes aside, Rojas believes that nothing is truly an accident, and every single thing we do in our lives leads us to become the person we're supposed to be. At one time he thought he had stumbled from his path by taking a ten-year detour as the Gorilla, but now he realizes that he never would have found his way without his time in the costume.

"I never saw the Gorilla as being my alter ego, but a lot of performers feel that way," he says. "You'll hear them say, 'Outside the suit I'm really shy, but inside the suit, I'm a different person.' But eventually I came to realize something: Maybe the real me *is* that guy inside the gorilla suit who was letting it all loose. And so I made it my ambition to live my life the way the Gorilla lived on the court. Why not live that out without the costume? With our kids. With our family. Really live without the fears and constraints."

So Rojas has one final question for you: "Who is your Gorilla?"

* * *

ON MARCH 26, 2013, the *Wall Street Journal* ran a story about Jay Horwitz, the Mets' vice president of media relations, who has been with the team since 1980. It was all about how he's a notorious "butt dialer," detailing a laundry list of incidents in which players have received random phone calls from Horwitz at all hours of the day and night without his being aware of it. It also made fun of his inability to use Twitter properly. "[Some of] his tweets have included such updates as 'Hy' and 'Congrats to $.' On March 2, [Horwitz] simply tweeted the letter *O*," wrote the reporter, Brian Costa.

One week before the start of the baseball season, this story was one of the most noteworthy items that reporters could come up with regarding the New York Mets—that the executive in charge of communicating with the media doesn't seem to know how to communicate.

Obviously, this wasn't news to me. The difference is that today, as opposed to in 1997, I truly no longer care.

I'll continue to root for the Mets on the field, because that's part of being a fan. And one of these days, I'm sure that during a visit to Citi Field, Mr. Met and I will cross paths. And if it happens, and he offers up his hand to shake or to high five, I will accept his offer.

His offer.

Him.

He's not me anymore, and I no longer look at him that way.

Mascots are indeed magic. But at long last, I've broken free from the spell.

ACKNOWLEDGMENTS

THIS BOOK WOULD NOT have been possible without the help and support of my family and friends, of which there are far too many to mention by name here. They are the ones who do it because they *want to*, and not because they *have to*. To my beautiful wife, Sara, who remains my first, my last, and my everything. To my son, Xander, whose youthful optimism and enthusiasm are a constant joy to behold.

To my agent, Jud Laghi, for championing the cause of this book for year upon year, never losing faith in the concept and making sure that I didn't either. To Christy Fletcher, for being so supportive early on, and for being so instrumental in the marriage of agent and writer. To my editor, Mark Weinstein, and all of the gang at Rodale Inc. for climbing on board for the journey.

To each and every one of the people who graciously allowed themselves to be interviewed for this book, both on and off the record. An extra-special debt of gratitude to Dave Raymond, for opening up his Mascot Boot Camp for a "peek behind the curtain" and for being so generous with his time. To the entire Ocean City Nor'easters and Lakewood BlueClaws organizations for the open access and warm welcome.

To my ESPN family for always setting the bar a little bit higher, forcing me to consistently strive to become better at my craft. To Tristan Cockcroft, Eric Karabell, Christopher Harris, Ken Daube, and Stephania Bell. To Pierre Becquey, Brendan Roberts, James Quintong, and Keith Lipscomb. To Nate Ravitz, Chris Sprow, Daniel Kaufman, and Rob King for their generosity.

To Matthew Berry, whose picture should take up permanent residence in the dictionary next to the definition of the word "loyalty." It's not every relationship that begins with the line, "So, we'd like you to wear this giant papier-mâché fish head." But it certainly set the stage for my life to come in more ways than one.

To all my Nickelodeon compatriots who spent time in the Gak Kitchen and on that Slime Stage. "Guts! Do you have it?" They most certainly did—especially Cailin McDonald. To those members of the New York Mets organization who did "get it"—at least from time to time—including, but by no means limited to, Mark Bingham, Jill Knee, Jon Rosenberg, Jill Grabill, Kevin McCarthy, "Behind home plate" Dennis, Chris Granozio, Sue Lucchi, Vito Vitiello, Marc Levine, Mike Kardis, Big Daddy Brand, Jen O'Dell, Brian from St. John's, and yes, even Tim Gunkel, who didn't always wear the black hat by any means.

To Carl Everett, Rico Brogna, Bret Saberhagen, Josias Manzanillo, Jose Vizcaino, Tony Gwynn, Jeff Blauser, and all of the other players who showed an interest and played along over the years. To Ed Montague, the only umpire to ever toss me from a game, for eventually coming around and becoming a fan. To Howie Rose, Bob Murphy, Ed Coleman, Sean McDonough, and all of the other announcers who took note of what I was doing on the field and gave positive on-air feedback more often than not.

To Rob Cesternino, Howard Decker, Corey Chapman, Bill Littlefield, Jessica Barton, D.J. Grothe, Derek Colanduno, Austin Tichenor, Robert M. Jarvis, Rachel Robinson, James Denniston, Gayle Lynch, Mark Schlereth, and the Wrigley Field Ambassadors.

And to all of my fellow comrades in costume, past, present, and future. Keep up the good work and remember my mantra: It doesn't matter whether you win or lose, so long as the mascot survives.

ABOUT THE AUTHOR

AJ MASS WRITES ABOUT baseball for ESPN.com's MLB Rumor Central and is also a contributor to the site's fantasy-sports department. His first book, *How Fantasy Sports Explains the World: What Pujols and Peyton Can Teach Us About Wookiees and Wall Street* (Skyhorse) was published in August 2011. He's a graduate of Syracuse University by way of the Bronx High School of Science, J.H.S. 185 and P.S. 214 in Flushing, New York—the latter two well within walking distance of Shea Stadium.

In 1994, AJ became the first person to don the Mr. Met suit since the mascot was retired by the Mets in the 1960s, and he played Mr. Met through the 1997 season. He's also dealt cards in an Atlantic City casino, performed Theatresports (improv comedy) in New York City, and even once got to "Sing Along with Colin" on MTV's *Remote Control.*

AJ lives in New Jersey with his wife, Sara, and his son, Xander.

INDEX

An asterisk (*) indicates a photo in the *photo insert* pages.